Bottled Up

The publisher gratefully acknowledges the generous support of the General Endowment Fund of the University of California Press Foundation.

Bottled Up

How the Way We Feed Babies Has Come to Define Motherhood, and Why It Shouldn't

Suzanne Barston

UNIVERSITY OF CALIFORNIA PRESS
Berkeley Los Angeles London

University of California Press, one of the most distinguished university presses in the United States, enriches lives around the world by advancing scholarship in the humanities, social sciences, and natural sciences. Its activities are supported by the UC Press Foundation and by philanthropic contributions from individuals and institutions. For more information, visit www.ucpress.edu.

University of California Press
Berkeley and Los Angeles, California

University of California Press, Ltd.
London, England

Library of Congress Cataloging-in-Publication Data

Cobb-Barston, Suzanne Michaels, 1978-
Bottled up : how the way we feed babies has come to define motherhood, and why it shouldn't / Suzanne Barston.
p. cm.
Includes bibliographical references.
ISBN 978-0-520-27023-7 (cloth : alk. paper)
1. Breastfeeding. 2. Breastfeeding—Complications. 3. Breastfeeding—Social aspects. I. Title.
RJ216.C652 2012
649'.33—dc23 2012010493

Manufactured in the United States of America

21 20 19 18 17 16 15 14 13 12
10 9 8 7 6 5 4 3 2 1

In keeping with a commitment to support environmentally responsible and sustainable printing practices, UC Press has printed this book on Rolland Enviro100, a 100% post-consumer fiber paper that is FSC certified, deinked, processed chlorine-free, and manufactured with renewable biogas energy. It is acid-free and EcoLogo certified.

For Leo and Lucy

CONTENTS

ACKNOWLEDGMENTS

This book would have been nothing more than the rantings of an annoyed new mom were it not for a long list of people far smarter than I, who shared their considerable expertise, bold opinions, and valuable time. For this, I offer my extreme gratitude to Polly Palumbo, Rebecca Goldin, Joan Wolf, Stephanie Knaak, Ellie Lee, Alex Tabbarok, Carden Johnston, Karen Kleiman, Maureen Rand Oakley, Dr. Barry Dworkin, Chris Bobel, Janet Golden, Dr. Michael Moritz, Linda Blum, Phyllis Rippeyoung, Mary Noonan, Tina Moffat, Julie Artis, Orit Avishai, Siobhan Reilly, and Eirik Evenhouse.

Much appreciation also goes to Katherine Abend, Christine Pietrosh, Nicolle Fefferman, Danny Bush, Jennifer Golub-Marcus, and Juli Schneiderman, who all read, brainstormed, and/or listened to me obsess about this project; my Pasadena mommy friends for accepting me into their fold despite my differing (and often unsolicited) opinions; my editor, Naomi Schneider, for her tireless tweaking and shaping of what was originally a rambling, somewhat schizophrenic manuscript; Kate

Warne, Madeleine Adams, and everyone at UC Press for bringing this book from gestation to birth; my unbelievable agent at Writers House, Rebecca Sherman, and her assistant Ty King; Brooke Linville for her support, Web prowess, and take-no-prisoners attitude; the administrative team of Bottle Babies for being my sisters in arms in a ridiculous and unnecessary war; my parents, Steve and Diana Cobb, for their love and babysitting hours (and my dad for his professional insight and access to medical journals); the whole Barston and Cobb clans for putting up with my insanity; the warm and loving crew of babysitters who've hung out with my kids so that I could write—Candace Rodrigues, Erika Kennington, Katy Williams, and Keewa Nurullah; Virginia Lam for her incomparable PR expertise; and the Strong Momma crew for reminding me that chat rooms—despite all their faults—can be supportive, positive places.

To the women of the Fearless Formula Feeder community who have shared their pain, humor, and anger with me, whose stories pepper these chapters and inspired so much of the prose, I am honored to be your "voice" and I hope I don't disappoint you too much.

Thank you, also, to the positive, open-minded lactivists I've met in the past two years—women like Suchada Eickemeyer of MamaEve.com, Devan McGuinness-Snider of AccustomedChaos.com, and Rina Groeneveld—who have helped me see an entirely new side of the story, and who I hope can read *this* story in the spirit it was intended.

Last, thank you just isn't adequate for my husband, Steven. Writing this book took a tremendous toll on our family, and I've asked way too much of you during these past three years. I hope I can someday return the favor, but until then I hope my undying gratitude and love will suffice.

Introduction

I'm watching an Internet series about pregnancy. While a new mom is being interviewed, her baby begins crying. She informs her husband (and the camera) that she's going to "go make him a bottle." A nervous glance passes over her face; it's almost imperceptible, but I can see it. The guilt, the conflict, the defensiveness . . . it's all there. And it hurts to watch.

Other women viewing this show will catch the moment as well, subtle as it may be. Some will grimace, familiar with the shame of being a bottle-feeding mom. Others will judge, wondering why someone held up as a shining example of motherhood isn't breastfeeding.

Before I had my son, I probably would've wondered the same thing. I had always intended to nurse my child for at least a year; I didn't allow the thought that I might fail to enter my mind. I didn't *want* to breastfeed. I *had* to breastfeed. Which is what makes watching that episode with the bottle-feeding mom so hard.

Because that woman is me.

As the subject of a popular Internet reality series for Pampers.com, every ultrasound, contraction, and hormonal rant I experienced during my pregnancy and first few weeks as a mom was recorded and turned into a romantic, ethereal version of new parenthood. Through the gauzy lens of the camera, a journey filled with fear and anxiety looks easy, complete with a heartstring-tugging soundtrack and fancy cutaways to the most dramatic moments of an often arduous nine months. But one scene, that scene with the bottle, rings painfully true and blaringly corporeal. No amount of editing could have softened the conflict I was feeling in that moment.

Six weeks prior to filming that episode, the filmmakers had been there to record my session with a renowned lactation consultant. She wasn't the first breastfeeding professional I had seen; no one could figure out what the problem was with my son's "latch," why the two of us couldn't seem to figure out what was supposed to be a natural, instinctive process. The footage from that day was never used. I suspect it was too uncomfortable to watch: my eyes were rimmed red from exhaustion and tears, my voice shook due to a major bout of postpartum depression, and my child was starving and miserable (later we would discover that he had a severe intolerance to all milk, even mine, causing him to writhe in pain and discomfort every time he ate). I imagine what they managed to cut together was more like a horror movie than an inspirational Web series. So the producers casually glossed over how we were feeding our son for the postpartum episodes, and other than that brief moment with the bottle, you would never suspect the hell we went through.

Besides the fact that my breastfeeding "failure" was televised, my story isn't unique. Whether a matter of necessity or preference, the way we feed our infants has become the defining moment of parenthood. Breast is not only best; it is the yardstick by which our parenting prowess is measured. Hospital maternity wards plaster posters with slogans suggesting that if you want to raise a happy, healthy child, nursing trumps both nature and nurture. Headlines announce new studies touting the superiority of children who are breastfed. The politics of pumping becomes a feminist issue, making any self-respecting NOW member want to burn her bra for entirely different reasons. Governments release public health campaigns imploring women to nurse for the good of the nation, and activists lobby to treat formula like a controlled substance. For many women of my generation, social class, and educational level, breastfeeding is seen not as a choice but as a given.

The day the cameras caught me "making a bottle," I felt pretty sure that, given our circumstances, formula feeding was the best decision I could have made for my family. But my intellectual rationalizations couldn't mitigate my worry. Was I condemning my child to a life of suboptimal IQ, reduced immunity, and psychological issues, as the "facts" suggested? Like many new mothers, I couldn't shut out the ominous voices on television, in the news, in the parenting circles both in my own reality and online; I had nothing to back up my decision other than a gut feeling and a few kind words from my son's pediatrician. Unlike many new mothers, I was a journalist specializing in consumer medical issues and the former editor of a Los Angeles area parenting magazine, but this only increased my anxiety: the sources I depended on in my professional life for factual information offered only vague, foreboding statistics on the detrimental effects of formula feeding. I desperately needed support from someone who had been through a similar experience, but I found none, save for some thinly veiled "I told you so's" from relatives who seemed to think my fanatical attempts to nurse were an insult to the choices they had made in their primarily formula-feeding generations. Between my lack of sleep, my confusion (my son was healthy for the first time in his young life, thanks to formula—so why did I feel so disgusting every time I made him a bottle?), and my feelings of alienation from the other nursing moms around me, things were pretty bleak.

So I muddled through. I surreptitiously shook up bottles of formula in the bathroom at Mommy & Me class. The chip on my shoulder remained securely fastened in preparation for any attack I might endure at the grocery store while buying my teddy-bear-adorned cans of powdered poison. I made it a point to tell all my friends that I was envious of their ability to nurse, frantically defending my choice, or lack thereof. *He couldn't latch; he was allergic to my milk. Yes, that's possible. Yes, it was devastating.*

Formula feeding is a guilty secret for women like me, women who read the news, worry about health, and overeducate ourselves to our own detriment. The more you know, the more bottle feeding becomes a scarlet letter of sorts, the mark of bad motherhood. We've all been told that breastfeeding is the nutritionally superior choice; due to its lack of accoutrements, it is also environmentally superior. Is it any surprise, then, that it has also become the *morally* superior choice?

Breastfeeding is usually a beautiful, mutually beneficial act between mother and child. But breastfeeding isn't necessarily the right choice for *every* mother and *every* child, whether it is for medical reasons, psychological reasons, professional reasons, or a myriad of other reasons that are, frankly, nobody's business. Under certain circumstances, breastfeeding becomes a painful, emotionally fraught, conflicted act. And if you find yourself in these "certain circumstances," there is little support. You're left hanging in the shifting winds of public opinion, during those first fragile days of new parenthood when you need reassurance most of all.

During my own days as a lactation-challenged Hester Prynne, everything I read portrayed formula as a last resort, sufficient but pretty darn bad, the Big Mac to a breastfeeder's organic salad. Even the can of formula itself pronounced that "breastmilk is best." I wanted reassurance that went beyond the sweet but ultimately insufficient message that we "shouldn't feel guilty" about formula feeding. That was all well and good, but I wanted *facts.* I wanted *science.*

When my son was eight months old, I began writing a blog about formula feeding, called FearlessFormulaFeeder.com. I wanted to provide a community for concerned, questioning, loving bottle feeders and to encourage the public to frame breastfeeding as an empowering personal choice rather than a government-mandated, fear-induced act. It turned out I'd stumbled on an unfulfilled niche—there were thousands of women like me in the world, desperate for the same sort of community, discussion, and information. I soon found myself completely immersed in the online parenting world, becoming the unofficial spokeswoman for formula feeding. I was far from fearless, but I put on a brave face for the women who followed my blog. They deserved it. Every Friday I'd invite readers to share their stories on the blog; these stories made my own struggle to breastfeed seem like a walk in the park. I learned about rare health conditions that made it difficult to produce milk or nurse without experiencing severe pain; anxiety disorders that were triggered by not knowing how much a baby was drinking at a given time; workplace complications that made pumping an impossibility, despite laws that supposedly mandated otherwise;

breastfeeding that brought up painful memories of abuse; micro-preemies who couldn't manage the simple mechanism of "suck, swallow, breathe" without turning blue. The more I learned from these women, the more a slew of questions kept me up at night (okay, to be fair, my infant son was keeping me up at night, but the questions didn't help). Is breastfeeding exclusively for six months a realistic goal when most women reenter the workforce (sometimes by necessity, sometimes by choice) after a few short months of maternity leave? What about women who need medications for depression or serious health conditions that are contraindicated for nursing moms—should they sacrifice their own health in order to give their children "liquid gold"? Should women with histories of sexual trauma or eating disorders, for whom breastfeeding might feel particularly oppressive or uncomfortable, be forced to bite their lips through six months (or more) of suffering? Is the antiformula culture insensitive to the realities of some parents, including teenage mothers, gay dads, adoptive mothers, or those in any number of other situations that stray from the middle-class norm? Why are we focusing so much energy on convincing women they *have* to breastfeed rather than offering better help to those who *want* to, and working to make formula the safest and healthiest alternative that it possibly can be? All of these questions danced seductively in my head, coming together for a big *Chorus Line* finish, the one singular sensation question that no one seemed willing to answer: *Is breastfeeding really so superior that it justifies the guilt trip we heap on all of these women, essentially scaring them into nursing?*

It took me two years' worth of interviews with pediatricians, researchers, academics, sociologists, feminists, statisticians, and fellow moms and countless hours of reading through medical journals, websites, breastfeeding literature, parenting books, and chat room discussions to answer these quandaries. I couldn't help wondering how much better my postpartum experience would have been had there been a book synthesizing all this information, one that lived alongside *The Nursing Mother's Companion* and *The Womanly Art of Breastfeeding,* which would have offered a dose of rational perspective and given me some context in which to make a truly informed decision on how best to feed my child. I couldn't find that book, so I decided to write it myself.

In the following pages, I'll present evidence that suggests that the benefits of breastfeeding don't always outweigh the risks to a woman's physical, emotional, or financial health, and I'll advocate a new outlook on infant feeding: one that refuses to embrace a one-size-fits-all strategy. I'll tell the story of a cultural phenomenon that has touched many arenas—politics, feminism, healthcare, science, and our personal lives; a story about how we view motherhood, how women view each other, how science gets bastardized by bias, and how our choices are not always simple. Each chapter interweaves my own personal journey with informative research, interviews with experts and other mothers, and contextual perspective, in the hope that my travels through the infant-feeding wilderness can personalize an issue that too often degenerates into assumptions and generalizations; that my own struggles and realizations can prevent other women from feeling inadequate based solely on their lack of desire or inability to breastfeed. I've chosen to tell this story in a manner that will, I hope, be useful to policymakers, care providers, and researchers but also accessible to the parents who are going to "go make a bottle" and feel terrible because of it.

Most parents are unaware that there is an "other side" to this debate, because the conversation has mostly been relegated to academia, most notably in the fields of sociology and feminism.

Joan Wolf eloquently picks apart the breastfeeding science in her 2010 book *Is Breast Best? Taking on the Breastfeeding Experts and the New High Stakes of Motherhood,* arguing that the body of evidence is inherently flawed and used coercively to support the stifling goal of "complete motherhood"; that breastfeeding "sits at the intersection of public discourse on science, health and personal responsibility." A decade earlier, the book *At the Breast* detailed the impressive fieldwork of Linda E. Blum. Through interviews with women of different ethnicities and social standings, Blum highlighted the social inequities that put breastfeeding squarely in the purview of feminism. A myriad of academic articles have taken the current state of breastfeeding promotion to task, provoked in part by a 2003 U.S. Department of Health and Human Services/Ad Council campaign that compared not breastfeeding to debauched mechanical bull–riding while pregnant. At the forefront of the infant-feeding debate is the Center for Parenting Culture Studies at the University of Kent, spearheaded by Frank Furedi and Ellie Lee; this notable group has begun challenging how the "moralisation of infant feeding" has contributed to the "belief that 'parenting' is a problematic sphere of social life."[1]

Yet, most scholars of the infant-feeding debate take a subjective approach, save for a few like the Australian women's studies scholar Alison Bartlett, whose intimate and fascinating book *Breastwork* focuses on the sexualization of breasts and the dichotomy this creates for modern mothers. I am eternally grateful for the skilled research and analysis that these pioneers have provided, but I hope to take what they have started one step further: by taking readers through the journey of breastfeeding failure, one step at a time, I hope to show the very human side of this debate. Breast versus bottle is not just a matter of public health discourse or a feminist issue, but a battle that affects women in the most intimate of ways—we cannot possibly understand the toll breastfeeding pressure is taking on women without hearing from the women who have suffered through it. If we leave the women most affected by this battle out of the discussion, by limiting it to the pages of academic journals most of them will never see and discussing it in a theoretical sense rather than a practical one, we may never come to a cease-fire. I hope this hybrid of memoir and reporting will speak for the scores of other women who wanted very badly to do the best for their children and found themselves in conflict about what "the best" truly was.

I begin, in chapter 1 ("Preconceived Notions"), by arguing that the current state of breastfeeding promotion sets women up for failure, framing the "choice" as one that is no choice at all and ignoring the (very real) underlying reasons that make formula feeding the better, or in some cases only, option for some women. I demonstrate how the "good mother/bad mother" dichotomy is manipulated as a way to encourage breastfeeding, by considering the emotionally vulnerable position most women are in when they start thinking about how to feed their babies, and by examining how a now infamous government-sponsored breastfeeding campaign brilliantly capitalized on this vulnerability. Other mothers weigh in on subtle—and not so subtle—forms of pressure and guilt surrounding infant feeding that plagued them during pregnancy.

Prenatal desires notwithstanding, once in the maternity ward, many mothers will find themselves smack in the middle of an inherent conflict between the "natural" discourse surrounding breastfeeding and the medical model that supports the actual practice of nursing our children. In chapter 2, "Lactation Failures," I show how infant feeding became the purview of the pediatric community, how this shady history resulted in an unstable marriage between breastfeeding advocates and the medical community, with modern mothers caught in the middle. Detailing my own inability to breastfeed successfully in the hospital, I also ponder if, from an evolutionary perspective, we may be evolving—slowly—into a state where breastfeeding is simply not as "natural" as it used to be; hence the need for lactation consultants, breast pumps, supply-boosting drugs, and so forth. We are often told that women in Western culture fail to breastfeed because of societal barriers, but further examination suggests that this interpretation may be limiting our understanding of real, lived experiences.

One of those real, lived experiences is that of postpartum depression (PPD). Recent studies estimate that as many as 20 percent of new mothers experience some form of postpartum mood disorder.[2] Chapter 3, "Of Human Bonding," focuses on women who have struggled with PPD and other psychological disorders (eating disorders, body image issues, and posttraumatic stress from sexual abuse) exacerbated by breastfeeding problems—myself included. I relate stories of women for whom nursing was somehow inexplicably linked to psychological stress, for whom formula feeding was a lifeline, a way back into the light—and I speak with a postpartum mood specialist who weighs in about the detrimental impact of our society's romantic notion of breastfeeding women, and the number this fantasy can do on the already fragile psyche of a new mom dealing with PPD. I also discuss how medications are determined "safe" for breastfeeding and how the complicated risk-benefit analysis necessary to treat nursing women with clinical depression is muddled by overblown beliefs about the dangers of infant formula.

Chapter 4, "The Dairy Queens," tackles the convoluted relationships among feminism, women's rights, and breastfeeding advocacy. Considering that the average American woman has three months maternity leave at the max, most moms have to pump their milk several times a day in order to comply with the American Academy of Pediatrics' six-month exclusive-breastfeeding mandate. We've turned into a nation of dairy queens, with political support for breastfeeding focusing primarily on achieving pumping rights for working women rather than on fighting for better family leave policies that would allow all parents—both male and female—to spend more time with their infants. I speak with a sociologist whose landmark study on white-collar breastfeeding mothers shows how lactation-friendly workplace policies can be a "double-edged sword," creating a goal-oriented view of parenthood that measures mother love in ounces of breastmilk produced. Through interviews with working women, I argue that even the most progressive lactation policies don't acknowledge the realities of pumping in the workplace and that a reluctance to supplement with formula is adding a third shift to the already stressful second shift Arlie Hochschild described in her landmark book back in 1989.

This chapter also questions why feminists have either unequivocally embraced or completely ignored the pro-breastfeeding movement. By brushing off the concept of "choice" as a mere construct of the formula companies (as many feminist breastfeeding advocates have argued), we have muffled the voices of women who may not want to nurse and have insisted that their feelings are invalid, merely the result of formula marketing rather than legitimate concerns about body and autonomy.

The title of chapter 5—"Damn Lies and Statistics"—alludes to the specific, biased, and often sensationalized information the public receives about breastfeeding. I question why certain studies have been so markedly overstated and others attacked or ignored, and I explain how breastfeeding research is rooted in circular logic and confounded observation rather than controlled studies or facts. A poor understanding of relative risk has caused us to view infant feeding as a key way to protect our children from harm and "maximize" their potential; it is no longer a question of whether breast is better, but whether formula will do irreparable damage. This overwhelmingly antiformula mind-set has ruled out the possibility of creating better options for the children of those who cannot (or choose not to) breastfeed—ironic, considering that we claim to be promoting breastfeeding as a means of improving child health.

Finally, in the sixth chapter, "Soothing the Savage Breast," I suggest how those involved in breastfeeding advocacy should reassess their goals and approach. The way breastfeeding is currently promoted and instructed ignores fundamental inequities in the daily lives of women in many parts of the world, and even within our own country. Breastfeeding needs to be promoted and protected, but so does the choice to feed our babies in the way that works for us on an individual level. Infant feeding's dark past cannot justify creating a similarly dark future, where women are forced, whether through emotional coercion, peer pressure, or political means, to breastfeed to the detriment of their own physical or emotional health.

To be clear: this is not an anti-breastfeeding book. I think breastfeeding is an amazing thing, and I've seen it work very well for many of my friends. But this book is not for people who are trying to breastfeed—there's already a plethora of great books on that subject, and more to come, I'm sure. This book is for the parents who wanted to breastfeed and couldn't; women who are conflicted about nursing and want to make a truly informed decision about what to do with their bodies; breastfeeding advocates and care providers who are willing to listen to the myriad reasons that women may choose not to nurse; and for people who are curious about the other side of this worldwide baby-feeding frenzy.

Mostly, though, this book is for the woman who is in tears, with cracked nipples and a screaming baby whom she can't mother because she is constantly hooked up to a pump, who wants so badly to quit breastfeeding and finds nothing but fear-and-guilt-inducing literature everywhere she turns. I hope that this book will help her understand not only the science informing the prescriptive advice in the infant-feeding wars but, more important, the context in which the research is undertaken, so that she can make a truly informed decision. I hope she will be able to find this book, buried somewhere among the seven thousand books about breastfeeding on the parenting shelves, so that this woman will have a legitimate *choice.* I hope that it will speak for her and others like her, a group that has been all but ignored in the ongoing, often one-sided conversation about infant feeding. I hope this book will help her sit beside her breastfeeding friends, free from insecurity and judgment. I hope that it can inform a discussion which ultimately allows all women to feed their babies with pride, whether they are nourishing their babies from their breasts or from a bottle held in their hands, and that, ultimately, all women will have the freedom to find their own formula for good mothering.

ONE

Preconceived Notions

After years of hitting the bottle, America has fallen in love with lactation. Breastfeeding rates are the highest they've been in two decades: by the most recent Centers for Disease Control and Prevention (CDC) estimates, a whopping 75 percent of new mothers in the United States are nursing their babies when they leave the maternity ward.[1] The credit goes partly to the researchers whose studies have shown a myriad of benefits to human milk, and partly to activists who have fought admirably for better pumping rights and hospital policies, doggedly working to make breastfeeding the norm. But the *real* heroics of the breast-is-best revolution happen not in government buildings or laboratories but rather in online chat rooms, playgroups, and prenatal classes, in the pages of parenting magazines, and in the headlines of daily news feeds. Fear of being less-than is a forceful motivator, and these days, women who do not breastfeed are portrayed as lacking—lacking in education and support; lacking in drive; and, in the harshest light, lacking in the most fundamental maternal instinct. From social media to public service messages and an overwhelming societal bias in favor of breastfeeding, mothers hear the message loud and clear: breastfeed or bust.

More than a decade ago, writer Tracey Thompson coined the term *mommy wars,* a "shorthand for the cultural and emotional battle zone we land in the minute we become mothers."[2] Thompson's war was between working and stay-at-home moms, and I certainly witnessed this struggle within my own family—my mom stayed at home, my aunt was a successful professional, and there was a constant stream of subtle barbs about who'd made the superior choice. But although I can vaguely remember some discussion of work versus motherhood in my young adult social circles, it was only on the periphery. The whole mommy war phenomenon seemed dated, something left over from the early 1990s. Like grunge music, or flannel.

Flannel has recently come back in style, though, and so have the mommy wars. But while the fight looks the same, this war is fought on a very different front. A literal front, actually: those two structures protruding from our female bodies, otherwise known as our mammary glands. This battle is over our breasts, and it is causing significant carnage.

While pregnant with my first child, I was aware of the breast-versus-bottle controversy on a peripheral level, as if it were a war waged in some far-off country. I looked at formula from an unemotional place because I didn't foresee it having any real impact on my life. I'd read study after study extolling the many virtues of breastmilk, and I was entirely convinced that it was the only choice for my son. He'd had such a rough start—my body hadn't done such a bang-up job of nurturing him internally, and he was born with the ominous label of "growth restricted"—so it was the least I could do to feed him liquid gold, as the books called it, from my breast once he was on the outside.

I knew there could be problems. I'd read about latching issues, insufficient milk supply, fussy eaters . . . but nobody I knew in real life had actually complained about these things. Also—and I'm not proud of this—I had a theory that many breastfeeding "problems" were a result of women waiting too long to have kids; that we were a selfish generation and that my peers would just give up too easily, at the first sign of trouble; that we couldn't be bothered in the first place.

My husband, Steve, had a family friend who was due around the same time I was, putting us in the awkward spot of being constantly compared to each other in every way, shape, and form (especially shape and form—this woman had gained only twenty pounds during her entire pregnancy and had taught aerobics up until her due date; I had packed on more than thirty-five pounds and sat on my couch writing and napping for most of the nine months). But she had made it clear that she wasn't planning to nurse, that she might pump for a few months, but no more than three, and certainly no actual "breast"-feeding. She may have won at being the better pregnant person, I silently scoffed, but I was already beating her at being the better mother.

This wasn't just naiveté. It was judgmental, holier-than-thou ignorance. I was an unknowing foot soldier in a new mommy war, one with a strong and ever-growing army. To be part of the breastfeeding infantry, it doesn't matter if you're planning to work full-time or be a stay-at-home-mom, if you're gay or straight, if you're a card-carrying left-wing feminist or a Mormon with a penchant for traditional values. Instead, the battle lines are drawn mostly by class, and often by race, but perhaps most painfully between those who succeed and those who "fail."

• • •

If raising a baby takes a village, then we're screwed. These days, when a woman is expecting and wondering what to expect, she will seldom turn to a book, her doctor, her mother, or even a friend. The closest thing our Internet-driven society has to a town square is Facebook. Confused or concerned? Simply punch any question into an Internet search box and voila—thousands of answers at your fingertips. Who needs a physician when there's WebMD? Or friends when there are chat rooms?

The Internet hooks you from the start: women struggling to get pregnant find themselves lured by the siren song of TwoWeekWait.com, where they'll be aided and abetted by others equally obsessed with having two lines pop up on a urine-drenched stick. Later, if you're considering a home birth, you can hit up Mothering.com, where there are plenty of folks assuring you that this is indeed the safer, smarter option. On the message board I frequented while pregnant, women would post queries like "is this labor?" or "am I miscarrying?" prior to calling an actual MD. The danger in this, obviously, is that anyone with a keyboard can claim to be an expert; the World Wide Web has opened us up to a world of biased misinformation under the guise of "Web journalism." The Internet is a physician, therapist, and best friend but also your worst enemy, a bad boyfriend who treats you like trash but then shows up with flowers and candy.

Google *breastfeeding* and you'll find a minefield of information. In addition to articles supporting the vast superiority of breastmilk over formula, there is ample help for any nursing problem under the sun—breastfeeding after a reduction or implants; nursing your adopted child; even lactation for men (which, for the record, is indeed possible). But amidst the plethora of substantial, legitimate information, there is also a cacophony of foreboding, judgmental voices: "lactivist" blogs that compare formula feeding to child abuse; public message boards with calls to action—"I automatically feel sorry for the baby sitting in the cart in the formula aisle as their parent loads up on cans of the stuff. I feel like yelling 'HOW CAN YOU DO THAT TO THE POOR CHILD!?'" says one poster on a Facebook breastfeeding group forum;[3] diatribes from medical professionals and lactation consultants, using their professional credentials to validate staunch personal beliefs. Even a board dedicated to planning Disney World dream vacations devolves into a formula-versus-breastfeeding argument when a woman brings up the lack of nursing rooms in Frontierland.

When I first performed my own prenatal Internet search on infant feeding, I was surprised by the vitriol expressed in these lactivist websites toward formula feeders, but since the breastfeeders were in my prospective camp, I chose to ignore my sneaking suspicion that something was amiss. Plus, I admit that I possessed an embarrassingly classist view regarding formula. Better bonding, improved immunity, less chance of childhood obesity, higher IQ, reduced cancer risk—all this could be yours, simply by nursing. Knowing all this information was out there, I couldn't believe there was anyone who *didn't* breastfeed these days, other than uneducated teenage moms, those with uncompromising work situations, or those unfortunate women who were physically unable to do so (and according to what I had read on the La Leche League website, there were very few of these women out there—far fewer than the formula lobby and misinformed doctors would have us believe).

It was one thing if a legitimate medical reason, insensitive employer, or lack of education stopped a mom from nursing; but all things being equal, it seemed selfish not to breastfeed. I certainly didn't think formula was poison; almost everyone I knew in my generation was formula fed, and we all survived. But as another poster on that Facebook forum lamented, if we *had* all been breastfed, "who knows how much better [we] could have been?"

In my former life, I was more than immune to peer pressure; rather, I would choose the "alternative" point of view just to differentiate myself. But when it came to motherhood, I was a simpering mess, just waiting for the cultural zeitgeist to sway me in a certain direction. Because when it came down to it, like Prissy in *Gone with the Wind,* I didn't know much about birthing babies, and even less about raising them. If the smart, progressive moms were breastfeeding, then I would be breastfeeding too.

• • •

A few months before I gave birth, a package arrived at my door. It included a sample can of Similac formula and a ton of literature on breastfeeding.

My husband watched me open the package and raised his eyebrows when he saw its contents.

"Why did they send you that?" he asked. "We're breastfeeding."

It was a good question, with a rather convoluted answer. The International Code of Marketing Breastmilk Substitutes (known in lactivist circles as the "WHO Code") prohibits formula companies from advertising in any conspicuous way: "There should be no advertising or other form of promotion to the general public of products within the scope of this Code," proclaims article 5.1 of this policy, coauthored in 1981 by UNICEF and the World Health Organization (WHO).[4]

The creation of the WHO Code was inspired by events that caused the Nestlé company to begin to be associated with infant death rather than chocolaty goodness. The debacle began when Nestlé deployed "Mothercraft" nurses, dressed in white uniforms evocative of medical professionals, to assist new moms in the maternity wards of developing nations. The trouble was that these "Mothercraft nurses" were not nurses by any stretch of the imagination, and they liberally doled out formula along with infant-rearing advice.[5] Mothers were encouraged to use formula under these false pretenses and sent home with free samples; their milk soon dried up, as did the formula freebies. Faced with limited financial resources and, in many cases, a contaminated water supply, babies were soon being fed with diluted bottles of disease-laced formula. This caused dehydration, malnutrition, and fatal cases of bacterial infections and gastroenteritis from the compromised water used to mix the formula; breastfeeding advocates claimed that up to ten million infant deaths could be attributed to the proliferation of infant formula use in developing nations. Physicians, religious leaders, and activists banded together to demand a boycott of Nestlé products worldwide and to encourage the promotion of breastfeeding as the safest and best form of infant feeding.[6]

The Nestlé controversy was integral to the resurgence of breastfeeding in Western societies, many of which had become primarily bottle-feeding cultures in recent decades. It not only revealed that formula companies were out for the bottom line and apparently had no concern for the infants they were claiming to nourish, but also led morally driven scientists and social activists to question the formula-accepting status quo. Within several years of the Nestlé disaster, WHO came out with its famous Code, an outpouring of studies suggesting the superiority of breastmilk hit the medical journals, and an international conference was convened to create the Innocenti Declaration,[7] which could be considered the cornerstone of lactivism. Developed during a WHO/UNICEF policymakers' meeting in the summer of 1990 (held at the appropriately named Spedale degli Innocenti in Florence, Italy), this declaration outlined the importance of global breastfeeding initiatives: "As a global goal for optimal maternal and child health and nutrition ... all infants should be fed exclusively on breastmilk from birth to 4–6 months of age. ... [T]his goal requires, in many countries, the reinforcement of a 'breastfeeding culture' and its vigorous defence against incursions of a 'bottle-feeding culture' ... utilizing to the full the prestige and authority of acknowledged leaders of society in all walks of life."[8]

The serious tone of the Innocenti conference reflected a belief—inspired by the Nestlé debacle—that formula feeding was legitimately dangerous. It didn't really matter that what caused the deaths of so many third-world children was not the formula, specifically, but a slew of formula-handling-related problems (contaminated water, lack of resources); even in affluent Western cultures where these problems were practically nonexistent, people began viewing formula as a deadly substance. This mentality became more pervasive through the decades, gaining momentum through literature that frames risks in ways that the average person can easily misinterpret. For example, in her book *The Politics of Breastfeeding*, nutritionist and outspoken breastfeeding activist Gabrielle Palmer chastises the United States for its hypocrisy in claiming to defend the life and liberty of babies in a myriad of military conflicts, and then being unwilling to set "guidelines for the marketing of a product which could kill children."[9] The Los Angeles Breastfeeding Task Force website somberly states that "the practice of feeding babies infant formula . . . carries with it profound risks in modern, industrialized countries, as well as in developing countries. . . . [M]any are unaware of how the lack of breastmilk and the use of infant formula compromise the health and well being of children in the United States. These risks are well documented in the medical literature."[10]

The United States has taken flak for being the only "major country"[11] not to adopt the WHO Code. (Ronald Reagan's administration held out on the grounds that it restricted free trade. Score one for capitalism.) However, years of lobbying from groups like the La Leche League, the United States Breastfeeding Committee, and the American Academy of Pediatrics' Breastfeeding Section resulted in the United States adopting much of the Code in 1994. All this really meant was that the government informed formula companies about the Code and "encouraged" them to abide by the rules. Breastfeeding advocates attempt to police these rules, but it has admittedly been an uphill battle; formula advertisements are still seen prominently in parenting magazines and on television. But there have been many victories, as well—a substantial (and steadily growing) number of "breastfeeding-friendly" hospitals have ceased to hand out free formula samples, and formula manufacturers are required to print an advisory statement on their products explaining that breast is always best (but the formula you've just bought is an excellent substitute!). In other countries where the WHO Code is uniformly followed, formula companies are far more restricted—for example, they are not allowed to advertise at all. Breastfeeding advocacy groups like the National Alliance for Breastfeeding Advocacy (NABA) are working to encourage the United States to adopt similar policies. If this happens, formula will become part of a shameful club—the only other consumer goods in America that have these types of restrictions and laws governing their advertising and packaging are tobacco products and alcoholic beverages.

For those of us having babies in the twenty-first century, breastfeeding advocacy is becoming more like antiformula advocacy. Suggestions on raising breastfeeding rates focus on eliminating formula from our lives: What if we made formula available by prescription only? If hospitals went formula-free, only allowing parents to use it if deemed "medically necessary"? And this isn't just from grassroots organizations. Even the CDC, on a webpage explaining its 2010 Breastfeeding Report Card project, emphasizes that in our country, "too few hospitals participate in the global program to recognize best practices in supporting breastfeeding mothers and babies, known as the Baby-Friendly Hospital Initiative,"[12] an initiative that puts heavy controls on the use of formula in institutional settings—even if the parents have expressed no intention to breastfeed. But perhaps the biggest game-changer in the way breastfeeding advocacy is handled has been the concept of educating women on the risks of formula feeding *rather* than the benefits of breastfeeding. This has provoked a recent movement to trade in the old "breast is best" slogan for the new "breast is normal," although the sentiment is nothing new. "The truth is, breastfeeding is nothing more than normal. Artificial feeding, which is neither the same, nor superior, is therefore deficient, incomplete, and inferior," Diane Wiessinger, an outspoken lactivist and international board-certified lactation consultant (IBCLC), wrote back in 1996 in an oft-cited article, "Watch Your Language."[13]

In this context, the formula freebies I received take on a darker meaning. But even for those who don't fear formula, and simply feel strongly that breastfeeding should be the default, these samples are troublesome. The belief is that samples are simply too tempting for women, that breastfeeding is difficult at first, and having formula in the home undermines a woman's confidence in her own body. There have been studies bolstering the suggestion that outlawing the samples might increase breastfeeding rates; one small Canadian study found that women were 3.5 times more likely to be breastfeeding exclusively at two weeks postpartum if they hadn't received formula samples.[14]

At least in my case, an unsolicited package from a formula company couldn't undo all the subtle, subliminal pronursing messages I'd endured since joining the profitable ranks of expectant mothers. Every time I walked into a maternity store, I saw huge sections full of Medela nursing products; rows of nursing bras and fashions; special rooms for "nursing moms"; breastmilk "test kits" in case a modern, socially active mom had one too many cocktails and still wanted to give her baby the best nutrition; baby and pregnancy magazines that consistently had cover stories on how breast is even better than we thought before, and so on. Nursing was the norm, at least in my socioeconomic and cultural stratum.

Even for mothers immune to social pressure, the fact that respected medical authorities have come down so dramatically on the side of breastfeeding makes a strong statement. The American Academy of Pediatrics (AAP), American Medical Association (AMA), and American Dietetic Association (ADA) all recommend exclusive breastfeeding for at least the first six months of life, followed by at least another six months of partial breastfeeding. WHO takes it a step further, commanding us to nurse for two full years. Although the Office on Women's Health, U.S. Department of Health and Human Services, argues that "the marketing of infant formula negatively affects breastfeeding . . . [and being] given [an] infant formula kit [is] strongly discouraging" to breastfeeding efforts,[15] a stereotypically anxious mother would have a hard time ignoring these research-backed mandates in favor of Similac's prettily packaged presentation of bottle-feeding bliss.

The same day the formula package arrived, I also got a coupon for a free six-piece Chicken McNuggets from McDonald's. I don't eat fast food; I didn't run out to the drive-thru just because I could get something for free. I couldn't really understand why the formula package was any different. I did see one problem inherent in the free gift I was sent, however, and that was the enclosed reading material. I was media-savvy enough to understand that the pro-breastfeeding pamphlet included in my Similac-sponsored gift was just lip service, but obviously they were sending mothers a mixed message by offering free formula samples along with a small booklet of advice to help with all the potential problems we might face if choosing to breastfeed: *Breastfeeding is hard. Choose formula.* Message received.

There are other messages, though, received indirectly but just as powerfully. Shortly after I received that Similac sample, I found myself wandering the hallowed halls of Babies 'R' Us in a daze, agonizing over whether or not to register for bottles in case I wanted to pump somewhere down the line. I was afraid of what friends would think if they saw bottle paraphernalia on my registry; that I might be setting myself up psychologically for failure, or giving my baby "nipple confusion" (an inability to go from artificial nipple to actual nipple) as some of the breastfeeding books had suggested. I already felt a deep sense of anxiety and insecurity about motherhood; two miscarriages and a problematic pregnancy had rendered me unsure about my body's innate maternal abilities, and I was determined to at least get the retail aspect of the job done right.

There was a woman next to me, shoving several packages of disposable bottle liners (both environmentally and maternally irresponsible, I thought) into her shopping cart. She had two older children who were shoving each other, fighting over a push pop; her infant daughter was sitting unrestrained in the cart.

Next to her, a glowing, tall, blonde pregnant woman was conversing with her husband. "Grab those ones—the ones that say breastmilk storage bags?" she instructed him, as he reached for something on the top shelf of the display. "I've heard those are the best for pumped milk—no BPA!"[16]

I smiled at the blonde woman, my kindred spirit, as the bottle-feeding mom's baby started wailing.

Message received.

• • •

My old college roommate is Catholic, and we have a longstanding debate on who owns the monopoly on guilt—her team or mine. I'm the product of a long line of Jewish mothers; she has original sin hanging over her head. There has never been a clear-cut winner in this battle, until now. Now I am a mother. Game over.

The guilt starts early. You get five minutes of unadulterated, blissful excitement when the pee stick turns positive, but then it begins. What about those five glasses of Sangria you had a few nights back? Is your baby going to have fetal alcohol syndrome? Maybe you haven't been taking your prenatal vitamins as religiously as you should have been. Plus you opted for the generic brand over the fancy Whole Foods ones your sister-in-law recommended. Bad, bad mommy. We'll know who's to blame when your kid comes out with scurvy.

For the past decade, no conversation about breastfeeding promotion can escape the legend of the 2003 U.S. Department of Health and Human Services Office on Women's Health/Advertising Council breastfeeding campaign. The campaign most famously featured a thirty-second public service announcement showing a massively pregnant, attractive African-American woman in her thirties riding a mechanical bull. She falls off; the bar patrons watching are appropriately horrified. And the words flash on the screen, ominously: "You wouldn't take risks before your baby is born. Why start after? Breastfeed exclusively for 6 months." Another similar spot relayed the same message with an expectant mother engaging in a log-rolling contest.

By appealing to mothers' propensity to guilt and fear, the PSA assumed a few things: first, that the target audience was committed to a healthy pregnancy and a healthy baby; second, that they were committed to the nutrition of their children; and third, that they were committed to being the best parents possible. So we're starting with a group of women who are already nervous, probably overloaded with information (my living room was a veritable obstacle course of pregnancy and parenting books), and the host of a ton of pesky hormones that make us cry at something as innocuous as a rerun of *Saved by the Bell.* The campaign's creators were well aware of the impact these ads would have; one member of the AAP's breastfeeding committee claimed the campaign signified "a change to promote breastfeeding as a public health issue rather than simply as a personal parenting choice."[17] Even the slogan used in the campaign—"Babies are born to be breastfed," rather than the well-known adage "breast is best"—was significant. The Department of Health and Human Services (DHHS) intended the slogan to address its growing concern that breastfeeding should not be seen as the "ideal," but rather that formula should be framed as risky.[18]

Even if one were to accept the general premise that babies were, indeed, sprung from the womb with a breastmilk birthright, where was the mother in the scenario presented by this slogan? Rebecca Kukla, professor of philosophy and internal medicine at the University of South Florida, voiced these concerns in a 2006 paper examining the campaign. Rather than addressing the real reasons women don't breastfeed—reasons that range from histories of sexual abuse and body image issues to economic and physical constraints—the campaign "portrays anything short of exclusive breastfeeding . . . as a sign of moral corruption and bad character. . . . We can only conclude that DHHS believes that women can choose to breastfeed yet are failing to do so, not because there are any impediments to their voluntarily making this choice, but rather because they simply aren't willing to do the best thing for their babies unless more pressure is exerted."[19]

There was a ton of controversy surrounding these ads, which were pulled shortly after their launch (but not before they scared millions of potential, current, and future moms, I'll bet). They even caused dissension within the American Academy of Pediatrics. On a 2003 episode of CBS's *Early Show,* Dr. Carden Johnston, the AAP's president at the time, claimed that he was absolutely in favor of a campaign to promote breastfeeding but worried about the tone of this particular campaign. "We want women to be able to choose to breastfeed and do that for positive reasons and not feel intimidated or scared," he said on air.

"We are for the breastfeeding campaign and we want to encourage it and support it and we want it to be accurate and credible. . . . Pediatricians raise their children and support their families with positive nurturing experiences, not with scare tactics."[20] A rational and considerate point of view, to be sure; unfortunately, Johnston and others who shared his concerns were accused of being in the pockets of the formula industry by some on the other side of the debate, and these cautious, balanced voices were silenced.

• • •

The DHHS/Ad Council campaign marked a significant change for the AAP. Although it had come out with statements supporting breastfeeding in the past, the organization had been cautious not to alienate the parents it served. At the time the bull-riding/log-rolling ads were released, the AAP was still relying on documents from the 1980s that, according to one breastfeeding activist, simply "encouraged breastfeeding and acknowledged the superiority of human milk."[21] Then in 2005, "Breastfeeding and the Use of Human Milk," now used as the go-to for AAP breastfeeding policy, was released; it was profoundly different in tone, saying in no uncertain terms that "human milk is uniquely superior for infant feeding" and recommending that infants be breastfed for at least a year.[22]

It seems likely that the new, unequivocal tone was at least partly inspired by the dissent in the AAP's ranks over the DHHS ads—especially when you consider that this statement was written by members of the 2003 AAP Section on Breastfeeding, the same group that cried foul when its parent organization, led by Dr. Johnston, pulled the plug on the DHHS campaign.

An older Southern gentleman with a slow drawl and kindly demeanor, Dr. Carden Johnston is like the poster child for a homey, warm, idealistic view of pediatrics; quite a contrast to how the defenders of the DHHS campaign had portrayed him in the press. In the kindest light they shone on him, he was a daft industry pawn; in the harshest, a slick political animal willing to throw the baby out with the formula water. "Dr. Johnston . . . developed this sudden and seemingly urgent interest in this issue not via a last minute clinical review of the scientific literature, or even after consulting with the AAP's own recognized lactation science experts . . . his concern came immediately after aggressive, personal lobbying by representatives of one of the AAP's biggest financial contributors, the $3 billion U.S. infant formula industry," wrote lactivist Katie Allison Granju in "The Milky Way of Doing Business," a rebuttal to the AAP's actions regarding the campaign. "Johnston hurled the considerable credibility and persuasive impact of the esteemed American Academy of Pediatrics into an explicit effort to stifle the most ambitious initiative ever undertaken to promote breastfeeding in the United States."[23]

When I met with Johnston seven years later, his recollection of the events was less dramatic. "I found out that there was pressure to have an advertising campaign come out of the Office on Women's Health, which would use fear tactics to promote breastfeeding. . . . [S]ome of the things they were saying pushed the data to a level so that it was no longer credible . . . 'If you don't breastfeed, your child is going to develop leukemia' . . . those kinds of scare tactics were there," Johnston explained to me on the rare sunny day that we met in Seattle, where he and his wife live part-time. "Now, if the data that something in infant formula might cause leukemia was solid, the Academy would have to find out what in the formula was causing leukemia and eliminate that, and meanwhile, encourage everyone to breast-feed . . . but the data was not that strong. And [the executive committee] needed to respond, because the Ad Council was working hard on this campaign and were likely to get something out pretty quickly. I signed a letter saying where the Academy was coming from; that the ads should be more positive than negative in promoting breastfeeding; and I think it's a very good letter. . . . What we didn't do, in retrospect, was to involve a lot of our breastfeeding advocates before we mailed it. We wouldn't have *had* to change the letter, but they should have been notified and consulted."

As for the claim that the formula companies were influencing the AAP, Johnston says that "the formula company was monitoring the website [so they] were able to show me what was on the website before the Office of Women's Health pulled it down. So, is that influence or not?"

Certain members of Johnston's own organization clearly believed that it was. Dr. Lawrence Gartner, head of the Breastfeeding Section of the AAP, spoke harshly about Johnston when interviewed for Granju's article. "Some of us within the AAP have long suspected that the infant formula companies had this sort of direct access to AAP leadership. . . . Dr. Johnston's actions have revealed the extent of this influence more clearly than anything else I've seen. Many doctors within the AAP are very disturbed by this."[24]

Whether there really had been "many doctors" offended by the executive committee's actions, or if it had merely been the vocal few that comprised the Breastfeeding Section, is likely a matter of interpretation. It's tough to know where the majority of the AAP really stands, since you'd be hard pressed to find anything on the AAP website having to do with breastfeeding that hasn't been written by the Breastfeeding Section. Johnston spent about twenty minutes trying to explain the role of a section to me; basically, it is "a group of individuals [within the AAP] who are enthusiastic about an issue." The executive committee will then turn to the section when it needs to construct a policy on that specific issue; for example, the majority of information on infant feeding that gets filtered through to the public via the AAP website is written by the Section on Breastfeeding.[25]

I asked Johnston if those in the Breastfeeding Section were single-minded, and if this posed a problem for the rest of the organization; he told me I had it backward. "Those are who you *want* to have in there. If it's child abuse, sexual abuse, if it's immunizations, if it's breastfeeding, if it's safety, child passenger safety, ATV's—you want the enthusiasts in there, leading. But I think that passion sometimes will distort interpretation of studies the same as it does for me when I'm doing child passenger safety studies"—child safety is Johnston's field of interest, as a former emergency room doctor—"and I read a study, and I completely believe it. There may be some holes in it that I'm not seeing. . . . You know, you've got all this science, and then you have your personal biases and beliefs. Now, which one do you go with? I mean, *this* is emotionally correct. *This* is scientifically correct. Which one is stronger? When the science is hard, it's not an issue. But we're making statements *before* the science is that hard. So you're using experts interpreting the best data that's available." (Which makes me wonder: The statements of the AAP are considered the word of God by most American parents. If the enthusiasts are the ones writing the policy, and being enthusiastic may alter one's perception of the facts, are the rules we've been following based on little more than bias and zealotry?)

Johnston feels that it's a pediatrician's job to lay out the facts and encourage breastfeeding. But he also warns that when dealing with a mom "who's had emotional problems before, or guilt or insecurity," doctors should tread more carefully. "I think you would handle that a bit differently and let her ventilate some about how important she feels breastfeeding is, and about her family support system. . . . How much does she *want* to breastfeed? And then, support her decision. I think a pediatrician still can approach each parent, each situation differently."

In practice, most pediatricians (at least the good ones) are probably taking this type of approach. I've heard rumors of a few rogue doctors in the Los Angeles area who won't accept patients who aren't breastfed, but on average, physicians seem to share Johnston's moderate modus operandi. Several studies have been conducted examining pediatricians' attitudes toward breastfeeding advocacy, and most conclude that pediatricians aren't pushing breastfeeding as much as the AAP official policy suggests they should. In a 1999 survey of more than fifteen hundred fellows of the AAP, "only 37% recommended breastfeeding for 1 year . . . [and a] majority of pediatricians agreed with or had a neutral opinion about the statement that breastfeeding and formula-feeding are equally acceptable methods for feeding infants."[26] (Interestingly, the same study also found that physicians—presumably the female ones—who had themselves breastfed were "more informed and confident in their [breastfeeding] management abilities" and suggested that "educational programs also be targeted to professionals to effect changes in their personal behavior." I wonder how female physicians would react to being told that what they do with their breasts is integral to the well-being of their patients. Or if the same type of approach were taken with the obesity epidemic, and the AAP sponsored weekly weigh-ins to ensure that its members were leading by example.) And while government and media support for breastfeeding has increased since 1999, and the AAP has issued stronger and stronger statements supporting the process in recent years, a study conducted in 2004 found that pediatrician support for breastfeeding had actually *declined*. Compared to a comparable study in 1995, pediatricians were "less likely to believe that the benefits of breast-feeding outweigh the difficulties or inconvenience . . . fewer believed that almost all mothers are able to breastfeed successfully . . . [and] more pediatricians reported reasons to recommend against breast-feeding."[27] Since the DHHS campaign fiasco occurred in 2003, I wonder if these changes reflected an underlying backlash against the extreme sentiments voiced in the campaign and throughout the resulting debates within the AAP.

Unfortunately, when doctors publicly speak out against the pressure to breastfeed, they risk their professional and personal reputations. After the birth of his first child, Dr. Barry Dworkin's wife was having trouble breastfeeding. The Canadian family practitioner came home one evening and found his wife in tears because a lactation consultant she had called for advice had "essentially told her that she was endangering our child's life because she was not breastfeeding properly, or breastfeeding enough, [that] supplementing was harmful to our baby."

This personal experience, and hearing similar horror stories from his patients, led Dworkin to write a column for his local paper titled "The Hazards of Breastfeeding." "In my practice, I observe many mothers equating breastfeeding to their competency to be good mothers. This narrowed perspective—the dependency upon one aspect of newborn care—can be damaging to the mother's well-being," he explains in the column, which appeared in a 2002 issue of the *Ottawa Citizen.*[28] "Despite the best of intentions, women are bombarded with messages that lead them to believe if they stray from breastfeeding they are potentially harming their newborn child. . . . There must be a balanced approach to newborn feeding. If a mother is unable to breastfeed, and yes this does happen, she should not be made to feel that she is a failure. . . . Every woman should be encouraged to breastfeed but should not be subjected to judgment of her maternal skills in a punitive fashion."

Within days of the column's publication, Dworkin received piles of irate letters, which called him "uneducated, unethical, and unprofessional. . . . I had people who felt that anything that forestalled breastfeeding was a criminal offense writing me, telling me how irresponsible I was, and how terrible it was that I'm an assistant professor at a university, that I must be poisoning medical students' minds with this kind of information."[29] It didn't matter that Dworkin praised breastfeeding as a practice, or that his criticism was centered on the pressure women feel to nurse and the dangers inherent in inflexibility, moral coercion, and misinformation. We've gotten to a place where you can't utter the word *breastfeeding* in a negative context without serious backlash.

Before I left our interview, I asked Dr. Johnston about his own family's experiences with breastfeeding. He told me that his wife had nursed their two daughters, but that her milk had never come in with their first child. "Our first kid didn't get any milk, so at the end of a week he was underweight. We gave him formula, and the kid caught up," he said casually as I gathered my things together.

"Oh, and that son now is a breastfeeding advocate. He works for UNICEF in Africa and does emergency nutrition. He got interviewed for *Voice of America* the other day about Breastfeeding Week."

A champion of breastfeeding, sprung from the loins of the man whom *Mothering Magazine* accused of "dismissing breastfeeding advocates"?[30] I can only imagine how Thanksgiving dinner went down at the Johnston household in 2003.

• • •

The ad industry certainly didn't give birth to the concept of mother guilt. Advertising just capitalizes on feelings that are a natural part of motherhood. Mainstream breastfeeding advocacy has acknowledged the power of these emotions as a valuable tool for increasing breastfeeding rates—albeit in a quiet, underlying sort of way. Sociologist Elizabeth Murphy has argued that government breastfeeding policy in the United Kingdom has relied on a sort of "quiet coercion," a phenomenon quite similar to what is happening here, on the other side of the pond. "Forcing women to breast feed would be unthinkable as an illegitimate incursion into the privacy of family life and an assault on mothers' autonomy and self-determination," Murphy suggests. Instead, by promoting breastfeeding as a way to better the health of the nation, the government encourages us to think and behave in certain ways, and to judge others accordingly; in effect, we are policing ourselves. "While experts are not, in the end, able to control how mothers feed their babies, they do set the standards by which women may be judged by others and, perhaps most importantly, judge themselves."[31] (The late Frank Oski, M.D., perhaps the most prominent physician breastfeeding advocate of the twentieth century, once alluded to this same useful tactic, stating that "if the truth makes mothers feel guilty and they develop some anxiety, perhaps the discomfort will tip the scales in favor of breastfeeding.")[32]

Murphy's theory might explain why being pregnant is tantamount to wearing a "kick me" sign on your back—or, rather, a "give me your unsolicited opinion" sign. That big belly gives strangers the license to weigh in on a number of things that seem entirely irrelevant to anyone other than you and your gestating fetus, and breastfeeding tops that list. One of my clients asked me in the midst of an eight-person meeting if I had started "toughening up my nipples" in preparation for Leo's arrival. At the time, I was just uncomfortable with her talking about my nipple activities in front of professional colleagues, but she also made the assumption that I was planning on nursing. As if it was unthinkable that I would be doing anything but.

There was also subtle pressure—the random older woman in a restaurant who asked me if I would be breastfeeding; the infant care classes where formula feeding wasn't even mentioned; the nurse on my maternity ward tour who warned us that we'd be woken up every two hours to nurse, and asked for a show of hands: how many in the group were going to be breastfeeding? (Needless to say, all hands shot up.)

These experiences weren't particularly unique, or even that bad in the scheme of things. Jennifer, who teaches at a prestigious Los Angeles private school, was told by a student's dad that he "wouldn't respect her as a woman" if she didn't breastfeed. (He delivered this gem during a parent-teacher conference, no less. Bet that didn't help his kid's grade.) Nurse practitioner Shannon endured months of chastising from her peers when she confessed she was planning on formula feeding. "I did not expect to get the flak I did from other medical professionals—none of which are my personal physicians—about my decision not to breastfeed," she lamented. "I was told multiple times, 'Oh, why don't you just pump for a month?' 'Why won't you breastfeed, it's the BEST thing you can do for your baby,' 'It's such a great bonding experience,' 'You will regret not doing this.' "

I spoke with a young mother who finally decided to "swallow [her] pride" and enroll in WIC (the Women, Infants, and Children program, a government assistance plan the mission of which is to insure proper nutrition for low-income mothers and their children) when she was six months pregnant. "During intake I got asked if I was going to breastfeed. I said no, that as a sexual abuse survivor I was uncomfortable with it. . . . [M]y breasts had been used in my attack, and to do so was to feel like I was molesting my child, to feel like I had no control over my body as it was being used in service for others. The [licensed practical nurse] told me that if I *really* loved my baby, I would breastfeed." She recounts that several of her WIC counselors told her that "they 'knew' lots of women who had been raped who breastfed," and suggested that since she had obviously had sex to conceive a child since being attacked, she was sufficiently healed to nurse that child.

Most of the women I've interviewed cite their own previous judgment of formula feeders as an ironic reminder of how powerful the "good mothers breastfeed" meme really is. "I studied the breastfeeding failures of friends and family. . . . I assumed they were lazy. I assumed they didn't try hard enough. I believed everything I read in breastfeeding literature as though it were the gospel truth," says Kelli, whose son was ultimately unable to latch, causing jaundice and insufficient weight gain. A mom of twins had felt sure that " 'good' mothers breastfed their children," and admits she "bask[ed] in the praise I received when someone asked if I was planning on breastfeeding and I answered 'of course.' "

"It's almost like with something like circumcision, or 'crying it out,' there's an understanding that multiple views are okay, but with breastfeeding we have reached a point where alternative viewpoints are considered uneducated or wrong," says Stephanie Knaak, a Canadian sociologist who has written several well-regarded papers on the infant feeding discourse. "There's a whole stream of thought that breastfeeding is natural and it's for bonding and it's this kind of wonderful mother-child relationship thing, and so it's good in that way. And there's the medical sciences aspect—we know that breastfeeding is very strong from a nutritional standpoint, and it protects your baby, it makes them healthy, and it makes mothers healthy. And then you've also got a public shifting of views about motherhood—that a good mother is the mother who does everything for her child. . . . [M]othering is supposed to be labor intensive, self sacrificing. Breastfeeding fits in very nicely with that idea. All of these different forces culminate into the same thing, and it makes it a particularly intense pressure. There aren't really any forces that speak against it."[33]

On the many lactivist blogs and Twitter feeds I followed while researching this book, the words of Eleanor Roosevelt would be thrown around like paper airplanes in a fourth-grade classroom—inappropriately and haphazardly, and often hitting unintended targets. Although Eleanor's original verbiage involved inferiority, not guilt, the (mis)quote most often used when the subject of guilt and infant feeding arises is that "nobody can make you feel guilty without your consent." In context, this quote often coincided with the argument that women feel guilty only because they know they have something to feel guilty about. In other words, it's a good thing they feel guilty about how they are feeding their kids because they have royally mucked it up.

What the people who use this argument don't seem to understand is that the most powerful motivator for breastfeeding is not peer pressure, fear, obedience, or any other "quiet coercion." It's *desire.* The desire to be everything your coveted child needs; the desire to have that indelible bond with the human you created; the desire to provide sustenance from your very being. And when for whatever reason this desire goes unfulfilled, the resulting emotion is often guilt—not because we feel like we *did* something wrong but because we feel there must *be* something fundamentally, awfully wrong with us, to be unable to perform this most basic of human functions.

In one oddly worded article, Dr. Jack Newman, author of *The Ultimate Breastfeeding Book of Answers,* writes that the concept of mother guilt is just another ploy of breastfeeding detractors; that we should not stop promoting breastfeeding just because it makes women feel guilty. "Who does feel guilty about breastfeeding?" he asks. "Not the women who make an informed choice to bottle feed. It is the woman who wanted to breastfeed, who tried, but was unable to breastfeed who feels guilt."[34]

Awkward phrasing and intention aside, those last two sentences are the truest things I've ever read about breastfeeding. I didn't find this article until I was six months postpartum, but I wish I had come across it during those rosy, innocent prenatal wanderings through the World Wide Web. Maybe it would've given me some warning about what was to come.

• • •

I had been writing for a popular health and wellness website prior to my son's birth, and the founder of the site had lent me a few books on the psychology of newborns. One had described how, if an infant is placed on the mother's belly immediately after birth, he will instinctively claw his way up to her breasts and latch right on. It seemed so primal, this preprogrammed knowledge, an instinct to both forage for food and seek comfort. I couldn't wait to see it in action.

To my obvious pleasure and relief, my first moments with my son Leo went exactly as the book described. His tiny movements up the outside of my stomach were like reverse echoes of what he had been doing on the inside for the past months. Familiar but hyperreal; I couldn't reconcile this small being on my skin as the same creature that had been cohabitating with my internal organs. It was disconcerting. His big eyes looked up at me as he pushed his damp head into my rib cage; the nurse shoved him roughly up toward my nipple and he found his target. It was exhilarating. The books hadn't lied. The nurse told me Leo was a nursing pro, that we were doing just great. I believed her.

Later, I was wheeled up to the maternity ward. There was a bassinet in our room with a baby in it. My long-awaited, desperately wanted, beautiful, healthy baby. He was a good baby—quiet, alert, an "old soul," according to my father.

He was perfect. For about three hours.

And then he got hungry.

TWO

Lactation Failures

There's a startling disjunction between how breastfeeding is presented—as a natural, instinctual act that is seldom sullied by physical or emotional impediments—and the actual lived reality of most early breastfeeding experiences. This has created a breeding ground for serious problems, where lactation "failure" is mishandled, misdiagnosed, and misinterpreted. The true failure, however, may be on the part of well-meaning but dogmatic care providers who refuse to acknowledge that legitimate lactation problems can and do exist.

Like many women, my initiation into breastfeeding was exceedingly technical, supervised, and regimented. During our time in the hospital, I was visited by three different lactation professionals (a mammary-centric version of the three wise men—instead of frankincense and myrrh, this holy trinity brought lanolin and breast pads), all of whom approached our breastfeeding "dyad" as if it were not a living, breathing mother and child, but rather two disembodied nipples and a free-floating tiny mouth. I welcomed these clinical ministrations, though, because despite a brilliant opening-night performance, our breastfeeding relationship had quickly deteriorated. If breastfeeding was a dance, Leo seemed to have forgotten his steps and I had two left feet. Or at least one left *breast* that functioned, and a right one that refused to cooperate—I apparently had some vague form of "nerve damage" that caused severe pain to shoot through the right side of my body whenever Leo would suck. Adding insult to (literal) injury, my infant son refused to latch on to the "good" breast, repeatedly pulling off of it and screaming as if someone had stolen his puppy.

None of the lactation consultants could get my son to successfully latch. The excuses ranged from a kind but vague "he's just sleepy, give him time," to the snippier proclamation that my new babe was "a slow learner." And although no one solved our problem sufficiently to make an actual feeding possible, every two hours, a clipboard-wielding nurse would march in and demand notification of how long Leo had fed and on which breast, and how many diapers he'd soiled. (I realize these nurses were just doing their job, but at the time I could have killed them all, even if it meant ripping out all my stitches to get out of bed and bash them over the head with one of those stupid clipboards.)

Considering how overtly medicalized the breastfeeding experience has become for most of us, it's ironic that the discourse around infant feeding so often coincides with an anti-interventionist approach to childbirth. Aside from the Nestlé scandal, a large part of the resurgence of breastfeeding in the late twentieth century can be credited to the women's health movement of the 1960s and 1970s, which raged against how the current medical system was taking motherhood out of the hands of mothers.[1] At the time, breastfeeding was a radical, subversive act; now, it is professionally monitored to a greater extent than most pregnancies.

Breastfeeding has been politicized for a long time—most historians credit the eighteenth-century French philosopher Jean-Jacques Rousseau with framing breastfeeding as a civic duty, a way for women to support the health and moral character of the nation[2]—but it wasn't until the nineteenth century that medicalization of nursing and childbirth really became a significant phenomenon, thanks to a confluence of events. The industrial revolution changed the dynamics of American society: women, especially poorer women, were joining the workforce in droves, making it difficult to balance breastfeeding with employment. Wet nursing fell out of favor in the United States; although it was still a viable option for the very wealthy, it was not for the majority of working-class women. Infant mortality rates rose as families began to feed babies unpasteurized milk or other inappropriate substances. At the same time, pediatricians grew fed up with their specialty being considered a "lesser" sort of medicine than that of their peers, and sought ways to become more relevant as physicians. By taking charge of formerly domestic issues like infant feeding and childcare, they were able to kill two birds with one stone—they could reduce infant death and illness rates while boosting their professional cred.[3]

By the twentieth century, infant-feeding practices were the domain of primarily male doctors, who worried that the "highly developed nervous systems" of their middle-class female clients were not conducive to breastfeeding. In response, they began prescribing rigid routines and dietary restrictions for new mothers, and standardizing "well baby" visits and regular weight checks to ensure that babies were adequately gaining weight.[4]

At the same time all this was going on, infant formula was becoming a mainstream phenomenon. Pediatricians often designed their own versions of breastmilk substitutes to give to patients when breastfeeding wasn't working—not working perhaps, as medical historians like Rima Apple have argued, because of the bad advice and birthing practices perpetuated by these same doctors[5]—and, slowly but surely, capitalism took over. A few companies began marketing infant formulas to the pediatric community, which would prescribe these products to patients as supplemental "relief bottles" or complete replacements for breastmilk.[6] Women were increasingly reliant on physician expertise as the century progressed, and formula was seen as easy, modern, and possibly even better than breastmilk in an age in which progress and science ruled. (For proof of this, peruse any women's magazine from the 1950s. The ads come straight out of *The Jetsons.*)

Needless to say, the advent of medicalized childbirth and pediatric oversight of maternal duties, coupled with the commercialization of infant formula, is universally blamed for the dramatic fall in breastfeeding rates in the late twentieth century. But Linda Blum, sociologist and author of *At the Breast: Ideologies of Breastfeeding and Motherhood in the United States*, cautions against a tunnel-visioned interpretation of infant-feeding history:

> There is ample evidence for blaming the patriarchal medical profession and, in the case of infant feeding, their collusion with the burgeoning formula industry. . . . This story is, however, more complex than capitalist-patriarchal collusion. The medical profession . . . [had] humanitarian concerns . . . and was also acting in response to mothers' expressed needs. . . . They wanted freedom from the control biology extended over their lives, including pain-free, safe childbirth and birth control, and they saw medical science

> as an ally. . . . Breastfeeding failure was largely an unintended consequence, and it is likely that both working- and middle-class mothers were grateful to have a safe alternative.[7]

Regardless of why the medical model of infant feeding rose to prominence, by the late twentieth century most American women gave birth in hospitals and took advice from pediatricians about how to nourish and raise their infants. And this had some disturbing consequences. Women were often rendered unconscious during childbirth, for example; babies were relegated to nurseries rather than spending their first days in close contact with their parents; and, as Blum suggests, the confidence women had in their own bodies was typically undermined. The women's health movement stemmed from the fertile soil of this cold, technological approach to motherhood, encouraging women to seek help from midwives and other more "natural," antiestablishment care providers. Even today, the AAP and independent physicians are often portrayed as ignorant, "pro-unneCesarean"[8] (performing unnecessary cesarean sections) and anti-breastfeeding, in cahoots with the formula industry to perpetuate the need for "artificial" feeding.

Grassroots lactivists struggle with the conflict between philosophy and necessity. They blame modern medicine for the advent of our formula-feeding culture, and our fast-paced lifestyle for the severing of familial ties that have essentially created a generation of women who've never really seen breastfeeding in action. But these constructs have also been the most useful tools in promoting breastfeeding. The loudest (and apparently most persuasive) arguments for breastfeeding come from respected medical organizations like the AAP and WHO. Scientific research has provided ample evidence to support the perceived need for militant lactivism, and the highly "unnatural" Internet has made it possible for this message to get across to the masses, even those in areas where physicians are not as up-to-date on breastfeeding science. "Breastfeeding advocates often are caught in the odd position of touting the biological advantages of breastfeeding while at the same time . . . criticiz[ing] medical practitioners for not knowing more about lactation and for providing false information to women," states Bernice L. Hausman, one of the most respected scholarly breastfeeding advocates. And yet, "much of breastfeeding advocacy itself is indebted to a medical model of demonstrating the contribution that breastfeeding makes to health."[9] Contrary to the back-to-basics, mommy-gut mythology surrounding nursing, breastfeeding in the United States, Canada, Australia, and Great Britain is firmly rooted in this cold, blatantly medicalized version of parenthood. Jonathan Wells of England's pro-breastfeeding MRC Childhood Nutrition Research Centre even argues that infant feeding is a profound example of biopower, "techniques [that] include normalizing judgments which subtly define the properness of an individual's behaviour, the institutionalisation of knowledge through which individuals are objectified and devalued, and the 'panoptic gaze' which subjects individuals to continual surveillance."[10]

Unfortunately, we might actually *need* all this monitoring to make breastfeeding possible in the world we currently inhabit. In the same article, Wells asserts that "optimal breastfeeding as defined on a medical basis by WHO is neither 'natural,' 'traditional' or even, possibly, 'normal' in a species that has evolved to exploit 'short-cuts' in parent-offspring energy allocation."[11] Breastfeeding may still be the best way to feed babies nutritionally, but using the "breast is natural" argument while simultaneously insisting on the need for more medical research, expert intervention, and education hints at a different truth: maybe lactation is becoming an "unnatural" state in the society we live in.

"The propaganda tells us that breast feeding is 'natural' . . . that's what the word 'mammal' means, for heaven's sake. . . . We forget, of course, that while, as *Homo sapiens,* we still possess mammalian equipment, we are no longer repositories of mammalian instinct except in the most vestigial sense," writes sociologist Susan Maushart in *The Mask of Motherhood.* "What our fellow mammals 'know,' we must learn. . . . Breast feeding is essentially a vestige of a hunter-gatherer way of life. The wonder is not that it grafts so poorly onto industrialized minds and bodies, but that we persist in trying to graft it at all."[12]

Breastfeeding folklore invokes the past as evidence for the "naturalness" of nursing our young—"If breastfeeding were so hard, humans would have become extinct years ago"; "If every woman isn't capable of breastfeeding, what did we do before formula existed?" What women who couldn't breastfeed did before formula existed was rely on other women who *were* lactationally blessed; in tribal cultures, this was made possible by what anthropologists call "alloparenting," a collaborative arrangement where it literally does take a village to raise a child.[13] This is likely a foreign concept for those of us living in Western cultures. Many of us don't live near family, and our friends are often busy with their own professional or family lives. Paternity leave is a rarity, so mothers are left on their own with infants pretty much right off the bat. This puts a lot of pressure on moms to iron out the feeding issues, pronto, even though most experts admit it takes up to six weeks to truly get the hang of breastfeeding. My friends whose families were local seemed to adjust better to both motherhood and nursing—even if there were technical complications in the beginning and even if their mothers were no help with the actual breastfeeding (another reason cited by breastfeeding advocates as a reason for lactation "failure" is that we aren't getting guidance, and in some cases are receiving active resistance, from older generations)—than those of us essentially in the "orphan" camp. Having a screaming baby, bleeding nipples, and little to no sleep (all completely normal occurrences in the first weeks of motherhood) is one thing when you have a mom or sister there to help you through it; it's another thing altogether when you're in an empty house, alone with your fears, insecurities, and seemingly dysfunctional breasts.

Even so, there are Western cultures in which breastfeeding rates are exceedingly high. The prime example of this is Norway, a country once as lactation-phobic as America, with the majority of Norwegian moms bottle feeding in the 1970s. Through grassroots efforts, followed by an extremely pro-breastfeeding prime minister taking office in the 1980s, the country raised its breastfeeding initiation rate to 99 percent and its six-month rate to 80 percent.[14] But looking a bit closer at breastfeeding statistics from Norway, we see that although 80 percent of women are indeed still breastfeeding at six months, only 9 percent are *exclusively* breastfeeding, with the biggest decrease between three and four months postpartum (63 percent to 46 percent).[15] This means that six months out, 91 percent of Norwegian women are using supplements—formula, complementary foods, or juice—rather than following the advice of WHO and their own government health authorities to feed babies nothing other than breastmilk for the first six months. Maybe breastfeeding exclusively for six months is not a realistic goal for most Westernized women—even those who live in what the most ardent lactivists consider the "ideal" pro-breastfeeding environment.[16]

Yet the party line of breastfeeding advocacy in the United States seems to remain married to the concept that nefarious external forces are the only thing preventing women from successfully nursing. One high-profile lactivist group out of New York calls these forces "booby traps."[17] The theory is that we have become a bottle-feeding society, and both our popular and medical cultures need an extreme makeover to cement breastfeeding as the norm. If this occurs, then we can return to some mythical golden age in which mother's milk springs eternal. (I've yet to discover exactly when that age was. Wet nursing was prevalent even in ancient Egypt and continued to be until other supplements started being used, at which point infant mortality rates skyrocketed until the advent of commercial formula and the twentieth-century medical model of motherhood discussed previously.[18] Even the glossiest PR firm couldn't glamorize that history.) It's clear that women face many social impediments to successful breastfeeding, but I wonder if a thorough examination of how these sociocultural factors could be influencing our bodies might do more for the cause. Vague acknowledgments that there's a "learning curve" for breastfeeding contrast with the naturalist arguments that we are born to breastfeed, setting modern women up for disappointment, frustration, and confusion.

Even in the animal world, sometimes there's a need for instruction and help: nursing and mothering don't always come easy for chimps. John Wells describes the first zoo-kept chimpanzees to give birth in captivity as "showing no inclination to breastfeed"; it was thought that since they hadn't observed other mothers and babies, they hadn't learned appropriate maternal behavior, implying that instinct may be overruled by situational factors. Studies of different groups of chimpanzees found that feeding behavior varied between the groups, even though they were living in "similar ecological environments." Wells uses these stories as evidence that "flexibility characterizing the [infant-feeding] process is adaptive, allowing individual organisms to improve the fit between themselves and their local environment."[19] In other words, living the way we do and where we do may make one way of feeding more "natural" than another, as opposed to what is considered "natural" by others of our same species in a different environment. But I wonder if this process of adaptation to a "local environment" could also apply on the tiniest scale. Two women in the same city, who fall into the same socioeconomic cohort, could have two totally different upbringings, life experiences, needs, and desires. In a culture where autonomy and individuality are revered, it seems odd to ignore the possibility that what works for me might not work for you. To treat human mothers as though we are equivalent to zookept chimpanzees—creatures of instinct who just need to be taught the "right" way to act—is a little insulting. And not only to the chimpanzees.

• • •

By our third day in the hospital, Leo had lost approximately 10 percent of his birth weight—which, although certainly within the realm of normal (it's typical for infants to drop 5 percent to 7 percent of their weight immediately after birth, but doctors don't panic if it's closer to 10 percent),[20] was of concern in combination with a case of jaundice caused by type AB–O blood incompatibility (this is another somewhat common complication that no one spoke of in my prenatal classes—Leo's blood type clashed with mine, which ultimately provoked his body to produce excess bilirubin).

The on-call pediatrician told us that we had a choice: we could offer him a bottle of formula, just to help out until we perfected breastfeeding and my milk came in, or we could hold off and see if things improved on their own. She was clearly trying not to pressure us; the hospital had been attempting to earn the Baby-Friendly[21] designation—a nationwide program encouraging hospitals to implement practices that supposedly increase breastfeeding rates—and I could tell she was treading carefully.

The Academy of Breastfeeding Medicine's (ABM) clinical protocol regarding neonatal supplementation in the hospital is explicit that there are very few reasons to give a baby anything other than breastmilk direct from the mother.[22] The document detailing this protocol begins with a list of when supplementation is NOT INDICATED—all in caps, as if this was the takeaway message of the document, rather than the details regarding medical emergencies requiring supplementation. (Is giving a baby a bit of formula because the mother is too exhausted to wake up and breastfeed—item #4 on the "when supplementation is NOT INDICATED list—more detrimental than not treating a severely dehydrated newborn?)

Table 2 of this same document lists "possible indications for supplementation"—things like weight loss in excess of 10 percent, and "intolerable pain during feedings unrelieved by intervention" (last on the list but still there, to the credit of the ABM). Between Leo and me, we fulfilled nearly all the criteria. According to the ABM, I should have been given instructions to pump or use donor milk as the first choice, or at the very least given a protein hydrosylates formula to use in order to "convey the psychological message that the supplement is a temporary therapy, not a permanent inclusion of artificial feedings." (I assume this message is "conveyed" by using a formula that is prohibitively expensive and smells disturbingly like rotten potatoes, as protein hydrosylates do.)

None of this was explained to me; rather, we were simply given a choice: to supplement or not to supplement. I didn't know what to do. According to everything I'd heard, one measly bottle was all it took to throw us onto the path of breastfeeding failure. "Studies show that 'just one bottle' can be harmful to both the mother and baby by increasing the likelihood of serious allergy to cows' milk protein . . . [i]ncreasing the chance of bowel infection and diarrhea by changing the pH of the bowel . . . [c]ausing nipple confusion—having difficulty latching to the breast . . . [and] affecting the delicate supply and demand balance," the websites had warned.[23]

For each of these claims (other than the increased chance of bowel infection, especially necrotizing enterocolitis—which is a real possibility because formula is not sterile like breastmilk, but is not a common problem for most full-term infants born in industrialized nations),[24] there's a counterargument. A recent study out of Israel suggested that early exposure to a cow's-milk-based formula may actually *reduce* the risk of later development of milk protein allergies;[25] the concept of a "virgin gut" is primarily theoretical. But "nipple confusion," as goofy as the terminology was (I had this image of two disembodied nipples running around in circles, bumping into each other, because of course nipples didn't have eyes to see where they were going), made sense to me on a physiological level. The act of drawing milk out of a human nipple involved different musculature than drinking from an artificial nipple. The theory was that once a newborn caught wind of how easily he could eat from one of those funky-looking silicone things, he'd never want to do the hard work necessary to nurse. If my son took after me, he'd probably see the logic in that argument fairly quickly, and we'd be effectively saying sayonara to any chance of a beautiful breastfeeding relationship.

Nipple confusion is actually a matter of debate for some lactation professionals—Dr. Marianne Neifert, author of several parenting and breastfeeding books, has hypothesized that babies who suffer from nipple confusion most likely have other breastfeeding issues (latching problems, insufficient milk) to begin with.[26] There is some threat of messing with the establishment of milk supply if the bottle is used too often, but there are ways to supplement without disrupting this sensitive process. One option is a supplemental nursing system, or SNS, a tube-feeding apparatus that attaches next to the mother's nipple, allowing the baby to receive supplemental nutrition (either formula or pumped breastmilk) while still stimulating the nipple.

Regardless, the fear of nipple confusion, of deflowering the "virgin gut," and of formula in general have made new mothers skittish about supplementation, and I was no exception. There was only one factor pushing me toward allowing the bottle: the thought of having to stay at the hospital longer than necessary. If we didn't solve the jaundice issue I wouldn't be able to leave. I had attempted to be analytical about how I was feeling in those first days, and decided that it was just the claustrophobic, sterile environment of the maternity ward that was causing a grainy film to alter my perception. I'd be okay as soon as I got home, away from the constant flow of healthcare workers and visitors, for whom I felt obligated to put on a cheery face and act the part of the glowing, prettily postpartum new mom. So when a new nurse came on duty and asked us if we needed anything, I blurted out in a shaky voice: "We want to try giving him a bottle."

I could have sworn her entire face lit up. "Really?" she asked, as if this was the first time she'd been able to initiate a bottle feeding without facing contempt from her patients. Steve and I nodded self-consciously, watching carefully as she opened a tiny bottle of sterile, premixed formula ("closest to breastmilk!" the label proudly announced). She showed us how to hold Leo slightly upright and position the nipple for the easiest, air-free flow. I gazed at my child as his mouth closed over the bottle's nipple and sucked desperately. I saw his eyes open, and stare up at the nurse. I recognized the look on his face, an emotion too adult for a two-day-old, but there all the same.

He was grateful.

• • •

Although it might not appear this way to a hormonal, fragile new mom, the Baby-Friendly Initiative doesn't forbid supplementation out of cruelty. The practices encouraged by the organization are based on a belief that it is "a rare exception when a woman cannot breastfeed her baby for physical or medical reasons." If there are so few occasions formula is necessary, why make it readily available or preemptively educate women about its proper usage?

According to statistics, only 2 percent to 5 percent of women have physical impediments to breastfeeding that render them unable to adequately feed their infants.[27] On balance, then, one could easily argue that educating women about potential problems would do more harm than good, scaring women out of breastfeeding, when so few will be affected by these complications. But as Dr. Michael Moritz, clinical director of pediatric nephrology at Children's Hospital of Pittsburgh, points out, even if only 5 percent of women are affected, "You are talking about one in twenty of a *couple of million* women who give birth every year. That is *huge*. That's hundreds of thousands of women having problems, and not getting support."[28]

Moritz was the lead author of a 2005 article detailing the rise of breastfeeding-related hypernatremia, a type of dehydration that occurs when there is "inadequate transfer of breast milk from mother to infant."[29] "Hypernatremic dehydration is assumed to be a rare complication of breastfeeding, but recent reports have suggested that the incidence is increasing. The failure to diagnose hypernatremic dehydration can have serious consequences, including seizures, intracranial hemorrhage, vascular thrombosis, and death," the report states. Moritz and his coauthors looked at the incidence of otherwise healthy, breastfed babies admitted to Children's Hospital of Pittsburgh over a five-year period who had elevated serum sodium concentrations (an indicator of hypernatremia), with no other explanation for this condition than "inadequate milk intake." Within a group of 3,718 babies, ninety qualified as having breastfeeding-related hypernatremia—and the majority of these were born to first-time moms. Although these numbers mean that the incidence of the condition is only 1.9 percent, ninety babies hospitalized with a serious condition is nothing to sweep under the rug.

Moritz claims that these problems have always been around, but physicians used to be more likely to supplement when things began going south. "When you are not reacting until you haven't seen the baby for one or two weeks and the baby is still not gaining weight . . . and you are not recommending supplementation, you are going to start seeing more problems," he explains.

"There is a very high rate of women who abandon breastfeeding within the first week, and that has been a concern. Breastfeeding advocates have tried to reduce those numbers, [but] you are not going to reduce them unless you are able to support these women so that they can *successfully* manage breastfeeding."[30]

The fact that most of the cases in his study occurred with first-time mothers did not escape Moritz, who had his own bad experience with jaundice in his first child. "Can you imagine how traumatic it is for a mother who is trying to do the best things for her child, and then sees her kid get sick . . . because that mother couldn't make enough milk? . . . I mean, even if there are no neurological consequences, and the child's doing great—to put a parent through that five days of hell until the kid has to go to the emergency room and you have to then put the kid on the bottle, or give IV fluids . . . it's traumatic."[31]

Elizabeth, one of a myriad of women I've encountered who suffered from physical lactation "failure," would agree with Dr. Moritz on that statement. Initially, she thought breastfeeding was going well. "I saw the LC [lactation consultant] for about 2 minutes. Grayson just happened to be latched on when she visited—latched on, but asleep. The LC said the latch looked good; I just needed him to wake up to eat. And then she was gone. We went home from the hospital on Friday. That weekend, I breastfed every 2 hours, but Grayson never woke up or cried to eat. I would wake him up the best I could, put him on and he would suck some and would fall back asleep. Clueless me—I thought newborns just slept a lot." Elizabeth had no idea anything was amiss until her appointment with the pediatrician the following Monday. Grayson had been born a few weeks early at five pounds, seven ounces; his weight had plummeted to four pounds, nine ounces. "The nurse took his temperature—twice, because she thought the first time had to be a mistake. His temperature was 94.9 degrees—dangerously low." Considering a temperature this low was indicative of hypothermia due to dehydration, Elizabeth was instructed to take her son straight to the emergency room. She and her husband spent five draining days in the pediatric intensive care unit, watching their newborn endure catheterization and spinal taps. After Grayson was discharged, Elizabeth continued to try to breastfeed, pumping around the clock and taking medications and herbal supplements to increase her supply, but eventually turned to formula. At the time we spoke, her son was nine weeks old and thriving, but she was only beginning to recover from the experience.

In an article for the parenting website Babble.com, writer Taffy Brodesser-Akner relates the story of her inability to breastfeed sufficiently due to primary lactation failure—a physical incapability of producing enough milk, resulting from hormonal imbalances, insufficient glandular tissue, or other medical issues. When she contacted La Leche League for advice, apparently she was told by a representative that "most commonly, the reason for low milk supply is a wrong position or something [a woman is] not doing correctly. . . . [I]f I tell them it's possible they won't produce enough milk, they'll use it as a crutch. They'll give up. We want them to stay positive."[32]

What's even more troubling is that this oft-cited lactation failure statistic of "1 percent to 5 percent" seems to be based on vague estimates rather than definitive data. Some studies have even suggested that physical impediments to breastfeeding might affect up to 15 percent of women.[33] "To get at true biologic lactation failure, we'd have to look at mothers who got optimal support and care from conception onward, and nevertheless were unable to make sufficient milk to feed their babies," Dr.

Alison Stuebe explained during a discussion on the Academy of Breastfeeding Medicine blog.[34] Following that logic, we'd be hard pressed to find a better example than Norway, where breastfeeding policy is backed up by free access to lactation consultants and a ten-month paid (or twelve-month reduced-pay) maternity leave, as well as a generous leave policy for new dads. Although the six-month breastfeeding rate in Norway is an impressive 80 percent,[35] this still means that 20 percent aren't breastfeeding to the "required" six-month mark—in a culture where, as one Norwegian woman told the *New York Times,* "Women who are not able to [nurse] are very, very sad.... They feel like failures if they cannot breast-feed."[36] If there are no social constraints, no formula advertising or hospital freebies, and women don't have to return to work, why are 20 percent "failing"? Even within the first month, 12.9 percent of women in a large Norwegian cohort suffered from breastfeeding problems so severe that they required medical intervention.[37] Chances are that not *all* of these women were suffering from primary lactation failure, but obviously there are issues here that "ideal conditions" cannot wipe out, and a significant number of women—and their babies—are suffering the consequences.

During the 2010 Breastfeeding Summit, anthropologist and public health expert Nancy Chin spoke to this very point:

> Mothers across studies, across ethnic groups, and across social classes all cite an insufficient or inadequate milk supply as an important reason for stopping exclusive breastfeeding before 6 months. By contrast, among health professionals, physical problems that inhibit milk production are believed to be very rare, with only about 4% of women thought to have this condition. This is a significant disconnect between what science says and what women tell us.... Where are the follow-up studies that can pinpoint reasons

for this discrepancy? Implicit in the lack of follow-up is an assumed failure of women to use the right techniques in breastfeeding, that they are lying, or that they don't really want to breastfeed.[38]

The doctors and breastfeeding experts who believe, as Chin suggests, that women are lying are not random extremists on the Internet. These are the people who are supposed to be helping us breastfeed, helping us keep our kids healthy. If those in the research and medical communities truly want to help women, researching lactation problems, rather than assuming women are looking for an easy way out, would do a good deal to support this goal.

Plus, insufficient milk isn't the only reason that formula may be medically indicated. Breastmilk is nature's perfect food, but what if certain environmental, dietary, or medical conditions alter that perfection? Back in 1995, in front of an audience of the most eminent and outspoken characters on the breastfeeding advocacy front, researcher Ann Prentice acknowledged that contaminants—as well as a variety of other aspects of our modern existence—could alter the absolute flawlessness of breastmilk:

> Breastmilk has also been shown to be an excretory route for a range of substances that might be harmful to the baby. . . . These include viruses, such as human immunodeficiency virus (HIV); environmental and occupational pollutants, such as DDT, PCBs, and dioxins; components of the mother's diet that might be toxic or allergenic, such as trans-fatty acids, aflatoxins, and cow's milk protein; commonly used stimulants, such as nicotine, caffeine, and theobromine; and various drugs and radioactive compounds. Where exposure to xenobiotics jeopardizes infant health, difficult and often controversial decisions have to be made about whether the risks outweigh the benefits of breastfeeding.[39]

Prentice mentions HIV only in passing, but the advice given to HIV-positive mothers regarding breastfeeding perfectly illustrates the dichotomous nature of breastfeeding recommendations. In developing countries, studies have shown that formula feeding (due to contaminated water supply or lack of resources) poses at least as great a risk as the very real possibility of infection from breastmilk.[40] Further complicating the situation, women who are seen formula feeding may be pegged as HIV-positive; this could lead to ostracism from the community or worse. Therefore, WHO recommends that women in resource-poor countries breastfeed exclusively for six months, while taking a course of antiretroviral medication when possible.[41]

In developed countries like the United States, Britain, and Australia, it's quite a different story. According to the international AIDS charity AVERT, "the advice from national health agencies is straightforward: [women in developed nations] should avoid breastfeeding altogether because the risk of HIV transmission far outweighs the risks associated with replacement feeding."[42]

The message from the major medical organizations might indeed be straightforward, but the same Web page where I found this statement begins with an admonishment that "even in high-income countries, breastfed babies are less likely to become ill than those given replacement foods"; and includes a quotation from the U.K. Department of Health proclaiming, "Under exceptional circumstances, and after seeking expert professional advice on reducing the risk of transmission of HIV through breastfeeding, a highly informed and motivated mother might be assisted to breastfeed." One could argue that AVERT—which claims to be "the most popular HIV/AIDS website in the world"[43]—is simply reporting facts, but when you start by talking about the risks of infection to an audience of immune-compromised mothers, and end by suggesting that "motivated" and "informed" parents can breastfeed, the message is far from neutral. Since the "transmission of . . . HIV-1 through breastfeeding has been conclusively demonstrated,"[44] this makes a good argument for why we shouldn't be afraid to admit that sometimes breastmilk may be less than perfect. It may even be deadly.

Transmission of HIV through breastmilk is an extreme example, but there are less dire circumstances in which breast isn't necessarily best. Milk protein allergy (and its less serious cousin, dairy intolerance) in breastfed infants is relatively common; when this allergy is suspected, mothers are typically told to cut dairy out of their diets (often along with soy, nuts, eggs, and other potentially allergenic substances) as a curative measure. Yet, a Finnish study of one hundred allergic, breastfed kids found that elimination diets not only failed to reduce allergic symptoms but also were associated with impaired growth and altered nutritional status.[45] "For the last two decades a resurgence in breast-feeding has been associated with a rise in the prevalence of allergic diseases," the authors state. "Consequently, the question addressed in this study, whether to continue breast-feeding of infants with allergic manifestations, now arises frequently in pediatric practice. . . . [U]ncoordinated elimination [diets] may result in a risk of general nutritional inadequacy or in unbalanced fatty acid profiles and deficiency of essential single nutrients, which may even amplify the risk of sensitization." The study found that when the subjects stopped breastfeeding, normal growth resumed and allergic symptoms were alleviated, leading the authors to make the relatively controversial statement that although "breast-feeding may be beneficial both for the primary prevention of allergy and for support of optimal growth and development . . . we may conclude from these data that an elimination diet adopted by the mother does not reverse sensitization that has already developed into allergic disease. . . . [I]f control of allergic symptoms and normal growth cannot be achieved because of the many antigens present in the breast milk, prolonged breast-feeding cannot be recommended."[46]

Elimination diets are still being encouraged as the gold standard of treatment for food allergies in breastfed infants. But I've spoken with a significant number of women who avoided allergenic foods religiously for months on end, to no avail. "When I told our pediatrician that Aiden was still having bloody diapers and rashes, my doctor implied that the only explanation was that I must be cheating, or didn't know how to read labels," one mother complained in an email. The consensus within the medical and breastfeeding advocacy community is that since breastmilk is species specific, there's no way that a human baby could be allergic, or even sensitized, to human milk. But then again, our bodies do lots of bizarre things. Humans are a strange and imperfect organism and there is indeed evidence that babies *can* be sensitized to their mothers' milk. "More than 40 years ago it has been reported that milk allergic patients may also exhibit allergic reactions upon exposure to human milk and auto-allergy in cattle has also been described. . . . Recent data suggest that sensitization to human proteins occurs early in childhood, almost as early as sensitization to food allergens," write the authors of a 2007 study appearing in the journal *Clinical and Experimental Allergy*.[47] They performed lab tests that showed reactions to human milk proteins separate from reactions to cow's or sheep's milk proteins, and used controls that helped establish that patients were reacting to the breastmilk rather than anything "coming through" the milk from the mother's diet. This is only one small study, not by any means definitive proof that humans can be allergic to human milk. But considering the egregious lack of studies examining this possibility, it's equally unfair to say that the possibility of human milk allergy is nil.

When Amber Johnson's daughter started showing signs of food intolerance, she obeyed expert instructions to give up a list of offending foods. Weeks went by but the symptoms did not abate; since Amber's daughter was constantly in pain from ingesting a substance that inflamed her insides, she developed an extreme aversion to eating. "Experience taught her that nursing hurt. . . . She all but stopped eating and growing. . . . I was told by shrugging experts that I was simply doing something wrong. That this could all be figured out and she'd nurse happily—I just had to hang in there and keep trying. . . . The result of all this effort was a hospital stay, traumatic placement of a nasogastric feeding tube that would remain for two months, and occupational therapy to address her intense feeding aversion." Amber's daughter eventually was switched to hypoallergenic formula, and Amber believes that the hell they went through was completely avoidable. "I couldn't listen to what my daughter was trying to tell me. Instead I listened too long to voices that were not in tune with our unique situation but were fixated on breastfeeding as the only way, the right way, the always-best way."

In 2010, the AAP began recommending a vitamin D supplement for breastfed babies, in response to research that suggested a deficiency of this vitamin in breastmilk. When a pediatrician was asked why only 36 percent of his peers were advising their patients of this new AAP policy, he explained, "We really want parents to breastfeed, and if we're saying the breast milk really isn't complete, that you need something extra, then that might be an inhibition to breastfeeding. . . . So those folks who place a greater importance on having the breastfeeding itself . . . might elect not to do anything that would dissuade families from breastfeeding."[48] In reality, it wasn't that breastmilk was suddenly insufficient but rather that our current fear of skin cancer had reduced infants' exposure to sunlight—a major source of vitamin D. Instead of explaining this to parents, physicians chose to keep silent about the recommendations rather than potentially discourage a belief in the absolute perfection of breastmilk. This same modus operandi is what makes the topic of chemical contaminants in breastmilk so volatile. The fatty tissues necessary for milk production are repositories for fat-soluble chemicals; in fact, breastmilk is considered one of the best bodily substances to use for biomonitoring,[49] a way of "determining which environmental chemicals people have been exposed to and how much of those chemicals actually gets into their bodies."[50] Breastfeeding advocates are not fans of studying breastmilk in this manner, as a 2004 article in *Mothering* explains, because it might "be viewed that human milk is contaminated."[51] True, it's human nature to freak out about these things, and those who do would be missing the important point that simply because chemicals can be measured in breastmilk does not necessarily mean that breastfed babies are going to start glowing neon orange. But considering that many breastfeeding advocates allow the dissemination of misrepresented and misleading studies, arguing that women "need the facts" to make an informed decision, withholding these findings seems hypocritical.

There's a popular saying that floats around the Internet, attributed to lactivist Amy Spangler: "While breastfeeding may not seem the right choice for every parent, it is the best choice for every baby." But is breastmilk "the best choice" for *every* baby? This is not a question of whether formula is better than, equal to, or worse than breastmilk, but rather an acknowledgment that sometimes an alternative to breastmilk may, indeed, be the better option.

• • •

If you're staring down the long, confusing road of lactation failure, brace yourself for an additional challenge: parents not only are given little information by healthcare providers on what could possibly go wrong with breastfeeding but also are seldom given instructions on proper formula feeding.

The WHO Code (which informs the Baby-Friendly guidelines) doesn't explicitly forbid doctors from providing information on formula—as long as it's only on a need-to-know basis.[52] Physicians must stress the "superiority of breastfeeding" and emphasize how expensive and dangerous formula can be, prior to actually explaining how to use the dreaded substance.[53] A 2009 review of qualitative and quantitative studies on the bottlefeeding experience warns that "misinterpretation of the [Baby-Friendly] initiative could also lead to insufficient advice being given postnatally. . . . [S]ome midwives mistakenly thought that they were prohibited to provide active support for bottlefeeding mothers, even after the baby was born (' . . . we're not supposed to be doing bottlefeeding demonstrations any more' . . .). . . . When women do not get information from healthcare professionals, they are reliant on friends and family, and incorrect practices are likely to be handed down from one generation to the next. *Errors in formula milk preparation and handling occurred across all studies that measured this.*"[54] (Emphasis mine.)

Another British study found that although 80 percent of mothers surveyed received information on breastfeeding, only

47 percent had been given information on formula feeding.[55] Of these women, the ones who wanted to breastfeed but couldn't felt the most lost. Which makes sense: before Leo was born, we'd studied up on breastfeeding as if it were some sort of parental SAT, but for formula we'd only crammed for a pop quiz.

Despite the fact that the majority of U.S. hospitals are not officially "Baby Friendly," most of the women I've spoken to received little to no guidance from doctors about formula feeding. Partly this is our own fault as formula feeders; I think many of us feel so ashamed that we're settling for the lesser choice that we don't bother to press the issue with our pediatricians. So, it's off to the Web we go, relying once again on Dr. Google. The trouble is that Dr. Google tends to refer his patients to famous parenting experts like Dr. Sears, whose section on bottle feeding reads like one big advertisement for breastmilk: "Let me be clear—there is no real substitute for breast milk. . . . One of our concerns is that even though formula-fed infants appear to grow normally, are they really thriving? Thriving means more than just getting bigger. It means developing to the child's fullest physical, emotional, and intellectual potential. We just don't know about all the long-term effects of tampering with Mother Nature. . . . Human milk is a live substance containing live white blood cells and immune-fighting substances. . . . Formulas are nothing more than a collection of dead nutrients."[56]

This reiteration of how formula is inferior to breastmilk seems punitive. A parent who is investigating formula, one who is neurotic enough to research something that is assumed to be as easy as scoop-and-shake, already knows that breast is best. You can't Google *formula* without coming up with a hundred reasons why it is comparable to cigarettes and fast food. Even if you believe that formula is evil incarnate, if a parent has already made a choice, the best thing you can hope for is that *at least* that parent is formula feeding his or her baby *appropriately*—measuring the formula correctly, for example, or using the right water (boiled, purified, tap, etc.). You'd think that formula feeding would be simple, but I know some highly educated parents who've made egregious and entirely plausible errors. One friend's baby ended up in the hospital because my friend and her husband hadn't realized that you needed to put the *water* in first, and *then* the formula; they'd been doing it the other way around, which disrupted the volume ratio of water to powder. She told me that she felt like a moron, but it's an understandable mistake. Sure, there are directions on the back of the formula can, but they don't make it all that clear that the order of the mixing process is vitally important. In December 2011, we were cruelly reminded that improper formula handling can be deadly, even in America: a ten-day-old baby in Missouri died of infection caused by a virulent strain of bacteria that was somehow introduced to an opened can of formula powder.[57] Although the media couldn't stop talking about the "infected infant formula," hardly anyone mentioned the fact that certain techniques could significantly reduce the risk of bacterial contamination in young babies. For example, using small, single-serving ready-to-feed bottles with presterilized nipples—ironically, the type of formula swag often found in those vilified hospital formula bags—practically eliminates this risk.[58]

What about studies that show a difference between formulas, like a recent one that showed that kids fed hydrolyzed protein formulas gained weight at a pace comparable to breastfed kids, whereas those fed regular formula gained at a faster rate?[59] Or studies that show that babies with a genetic propensity to certain allergies fare better on a specific type of formula?[60] Parents have a right to know these things. *Babies* have a right to have their parents know these things. Rather than wasting time chastising parents for choosing the crap choice, we could be ensuring that kids are getting the very best crap they can possibly get.

A week after we left the hospital, we discovered the reason why Leo was never able to latch on correctly. The seventh lactation consultant we saw diagnosed Leo with a restricted frenulum, or "tongue tie," which meant that the little flap of skin under his tongue (called the *frenulum*) was so tight that it was causing mechanical problems with his latch. This was apparently so common a problem that in the past midwives would proactively slice with a fingernail the frenulum of every baby they delivered.

In its nonmedical application, *Merriam-Webster's Collegiate Dictionary* defines the term *tongue-tied* as an adjective meaning "unable or disinclined to speak freely." It's interesting that the dictionary writers chose this definition, because *unable* and *disinclined* are two markedly different words. One implies duress (you are *unable* to speak freely because someone is keeping you from revealing the truth) while the other implies choice (you are *disinclined* to speak freely because you are simply unwilling or reluctant). When it comes to lactation problems, it seems that being tongue tied, in all three of its definitions, is a prevalent and potentially harmful norm.

THREE

Of Human Bonding

When Karen Kleiman began her clinical practice treating women with postpartum mood disorders, she was highly motivated to prevent nursing moms from falling through cracks in the system. A former breastfeeding counselor, she understood the need for advocacy and education on a visceral level, considering that she had been mistakenly instructed to stop breastfeeding her second child after a breast cancer scare and subsequent surgery.

Shortly after giving a talk on postpartum adjustment issues to a local moms' group, Kleiman, by then executive director of the Postpartum Stress Center and author of a number of books on postpartum depression (PPD), met for a one-time consultation with a woman who'd been in the audience. The woman, Dawn, told Kleiman that she'd suffered from PPD with her first child, and now that she was pregnant again, she wanted to do everything she could to prevent a reoccurrence. "She was doing everything right—she had the doctor on board, the medication plan in place, everything seemed to be in order," Kleiman recalls. "As she was leaving, I told her to call me after she had her baby and let me know how she was doing."

That call came several months later, in the form of a barely intelligible voice repeating the words, "*Help me, help me* . . ." Dawn told Kleiman that she was taking a low dose of her prescribed antidepressant and didn't want to call her therapist because she was breastfeeding and was worried he'd tell her to increase her medication to a level that wasn't safe for her baby.

> I said, well, then here is your choice: you either increase your meds and keep breastfeeding, or stop breastfeeding; but you need to increase your meds. And she said, "I can't." . . . After listening to her wish to "disappear" and "sleep and never wake up," I told her she *needed* to contact her doctor and therapist immediately. She said she would. . . . She called a few days later, sounding terribly agitated, repeating the same things, clinging to the notion that any treatment intervention by her doctor would interfere with breastfeeding. I kept saying to her, this is the depression talking, this is distorted thinking. . . . You want to protect your baby, I know, but your baby will be better cared for if you take care of yourself. The next phone call I got was from the police who found her dead with a self-inflicted gunshot wound to the head, with my card lying next to her.[1]

"That was the experience that showed me something is really wrong with this picture," Kleiman explains. "This notion that breast is always best under any circumstance, no matter what, is killing women, and I now have zero tolerance for it. This is not about feeding babies anymore. It has turned into something way more than that. It's about trying to be a perfect mother."

The relationship between breastfeeding and depression is murky, and likely varies from mother to mother. Breastfeeding can be a "lifeline," the last string of the fraying rope connecting a depressed mother to her child. She may be unable to relate or comfort or connect with her baby on any other level, but at least she can nourish him. That's reason enough to protect and support depressed moms who want to continue nursing. But there's another chapter to this story, and it centers on expectation and guilt. When authoritative voices tell us that breastfeeding is the "most important thing a mother can do for her child" or that "babies are born to be breastfed," how can we not internalize this? For a mom who already fears that she's endangering her child's welfare due to her own crappy mental state, these concepts take on monstrous proportions.

As I struggled to feed Leo, that particular monster was lurking under the overpriced red glider where I'd sit for hours, trying unsuccessfully to nurse him. Each time I brought him close to my chest, he'd recoil in what eerily resembled horror, jerking his fragile neck away from me with impressive strength. I'd held tight to hope after our "tongue tie" diagnosis, praying we'd find salvation through a pair of surgical scissors, but to no avail. After the pediatric dentist had pried open Leo's stubborn mouth and cut the gossamer thread of his frenulum in one efficient clip, I'd put my screaming son to my breast immediately, expecting the angels to sing as we nursed successfully for the first time. But the only thing we had to show for it, in the end, was a ring of my son's bright red blood around my nipple. I still couldn't feed my baby, something that was supposed to be instinctual, the "most important thing a mother can do for her child," according to all the websites I'd read. But my son hated my breasts. He hated me. Who would blame him? He could probably sense who I really was; who'd want to drink any part of that?

To "just give him a bottle," as my parents and in-laws suggested, would be the easy solution. Part of me wanted to do it, so badly . . . just so I could escape into the sweet oblivion of sleep for a short time, so I could give my nipples, and my increasingly fragile mind, a break. But I couldn't give up. My only job was to feed the baby, and if I failed at that, I'd be rendered completely irrelevant. Steve was handling the parenting thing wonderfully—he was changing the diapers, cuddling Leo, talking to him. All things I couldn't face, for a reason that was becoming painfully clear.

I wasn't quite ready to speak the name of that reason; it wasn't until nearly a week later, when we saw Leo's pediatrician, that I was able to admit the truth. The doctor, a pretty blonde who was seven months pregnant with her own first child, examined Leo and then spent a few moments glancing over his chart. "How's he eating?" she asked. Steve filled her in on the details, putting a far more positive spin on it than I would have. He told her that despite getting his tongue tie fixed, Leo had still been having trouble latching; but we were determined to make it work and planned to meet with more lactation consultants. She nodded approvingly. "Okay, well, keep it up. He's lost a fair amount of weight, and he's a little guy as is . . . but his jaundice is gone, so that's all good."

Then she turned to me. "How're you holding up, mom?"

I wanted to tell her I was fine. I opened my mouth, intending to lie, to keep up the act I thought I'd perfected in the past few days. But the truth escaped somehow, the words forming on my lips before I could stop them, as if they were separate entities with minds of their own. Like they knew better than I did that I could, and should, trust this doctor, this woman.

"I think I may have postpartum depression." It sounded stupid, canned. It came out on the heels of a sob. My voice cracked embarrassingly. Steve wouldn't even look at me. I knew he was ashamed of me. *I* was ashamed of me. I was weak and selfish and useless. At least it was out in the open now.

There must have been tears, because the pediatrician handed me a box of Kleenex. "That's okay," she said, quietly. "It happens."

I managed to explain to her that I'd been on an antidepressant in the past for eating disorder issues, and that it had worked wonders. Could I try going back on, even though I was breastfeeding? My obstetrician had made me go off this medication during my pregnancy due to the risk of potential side effects to a gestating fetus, so I wasn't sure if the same risks carried over into breastfeeding. I was mostly asking for confirmation on what I'd already been told by the big Internet breastfeeding gurus—Kellymom.com, the La Leche League website, and Breastfeeding.com had all informed me that the risks of not breastfeeding far outweighed any minor risks from depression medications.

But my son's new doctor leaned against the exam table, looking distressed. "I wish I could tell you that I'd seen enough long-term research on this subject to give you a definitive answer. Can I say that there's no chance of antidepressants coming through milk, or affecting Leo? Unfortunately, I can't do that."

The doctor caught my eye, held it. "Your kid can still grow up to be president if he's formula-fed, you know. Better to have a mom who is happy and healthy. You have a choice." Bullshit, I thought, registering her pregnant belly. I'd bet *she* was planning on breastfeeding. I nodded my head, acquiesced to my fate. So that was it, then. I'd just have to live like this.

• • •

Our pediatrician was correct: at present, there are no long-term studies available on the effects of antidepressant medications on nurslings. Actually, there are embarrassingly few long-term studies on breastfeeding and medication, period. That's not to say that research hasn't been conducted—it's simply that since the medical and scientific communities have only recently begun focusing so heavily on breastfeeding, there hasn't been enough time to gather sufficient long-term research. Thus far, it's been determined that four factors measure the safety of a drug for breastfeeding: how high a dosage the mom is taking; how much of the drug is passing into the mom's blood plasma; how much is getting into the breast milk; and how much is getting into the baby's serum (which is basically the substance left when plasma is separated from blood).[2]

The best science can give us at this point is a "rating system," judging the safety of medications similarly to how it is done for pregnant women. The go-to sources who administer these ratings are the American Academy of Pediatrics and a Harvard-educated pharmacologist by the name of Thomas Hale, who has become the widely accepted final word on drug compatibility with breastfeeding. Hale's book, *Medications and Mothers' Milk*, is touted as "the most comprehensive medication guide for breastfeeding mothers, endorsed by lactation experts across the country. . . . [T]his manual of lactational pharmacology is a detailed reference book that compiles relevant published research literature and the AAP recommendations."[3] Hale also runs a website called LactMed, and most recently began offering a toll-free hotline that both mothers and care providers can call to ask personal questions on specific medications.

Some critics complain that too many doctors blindly accept the warnings issued by drug companies about use during pregnancy and breastfeeding, since these warnings are usually based on nothing empirical, but rather a "we don't really know, so let's not risk it" approach.[4] But Hale's method for determining safety isn't exactly perfect, either. He qualifies drugs as "safest," "safe," "moderately safe," "possibly hazardous," or "contraindicated," based solely on (admittedly thorough) research his own team has conducted or the few high-quality studies available. Hale is obviously a brilliant expert in his field (and seems like a genuinely good guy, from the podcasts and videos I've heard and watched), and he's doing a great thing for women. But it's disconcerting that we are basing decisions on one man's research, especially one who is admittedly dedicated to raising breastfeeding rates. (He also has a conflict of interest, as his publishing group produces breastfeeding-related literature and conferences.) The name Hale is used to back up nearly every claim on the safety of medicine. Consider this passage from the *Journal of Pediatric Health Care:*

> With rare exceptions, the concentrations of medications most likely to be prescribed to breastfeeding mothers are exceedingly low in breast milk and the dose delivered to the breastfed infant is most often subclinical (Hale, 2002). Therefore, in reality, very few drugs are contraindicated during lactation . . . (Hale, 2002). Furthermore, recommendations must take into account the oral bioavailability of the specific medication by an infant and the comprehensive clinical evaluation of the infant's ability to tolerate exposure to the maternal medication in question (Hale, 2002).[5]

This invoking of the Hale name isn't the exception; it's the rule. I'm unaware of any other field of medicine that relies on the work and opinion of one person to determine safety protocol, or that prefaces discussions of scientific studies with moral judgments. That same *Journal of Pediatric Health Care* article warns that "ethically, practitioners can no longer hide behind the notion that it is easier and less threatening to recommend weaning than it is to look into the situation and be assured that a particular medication poses little or no danger to the infant.... Basing lactation advice on documented evidence is the first step in acknowledging that breastfeeding care is not simply a personal lifestyle choice but also a health care behavior deserving of both scientific study and informed clinical assistance." And this wasn't an opinion piece. Likewise, Dr. Jack Newman acknowledges that "we don't know the long-term effects of antidepressants on breastfeeding infants," but counters this argument by noting that "we also do not know all the long-term effects of not breastfeeding."[6] Considering that we have several generations of humans who have thrived on formula, and have yet to see the long-term effects on infants nursed by mothers on drugs that have, in some cases, been on the market for only a decade, this is a troubling statement.

Everything I could find on this topic did acknowledge that there were *explicit* dangers to an infant consuming breastmilk from a mother who smoked, drank more than the recommended amount, or took certain illegal or legal drugs, but these were considered to be "outweighed" by the dangers of not breastfeeding. But here's the thing: the "dangers" of not breastfeeding are all based on observational studies; the dangers of the drugs/smoking/alcohol are somewhat quantifiable—for example, we can measure levels of nicotine or alcohol in breastmilk samples.[7] How these levels actually affect infants is another story; measuring the impact of illegal substances on children's health and intelligence would be subject to the same restrictions as studies about formula feeding, meaning that they would be only observational assessments. Still, there's at least a bit stronger evidence for how certain substances can harm breastfeeding babies than there is for how *not* breastfeeding can harm babies—so why is the discourse so dramatically different?

One of the most commonly prescribed postpartum pain relievers, a combo of hydrocodone (Vicodin) and acetaminophen, is given to nursing mothers without much thought. But as recently as 2007, one study reported that although "case reports suggest that hydrocodone in breast milk sometimes may be problematic for the breastfed infant," "no reports exist on the amount of its excretion into breast milk."[8] *No reports* showing exactly how much, if any, of this drug comes through breastmilk, and yet doctors are encouraging women to breastfeed while on these medications. (When I contacted one of the authors of this study, he also informed me that there had been at least one recorded infant death due to this drug passing through breastmilk, and that "much of the information that mothers are given on drug use during breastfeeding has little scientific basis.")

Hale has said that we actually have more data on antidepressants and breastmilk than any other type of medication,[9] but to judge from the notes on a keynote address he made on the subject at a 2002 La Leche League conference,[10] "more" doesn't exactly mean sufficient. When discussing Zoloft as the "best drug choice so far," he used as evidence an "excellent study of 11 mother/infant pairs." *Eleven pairs.* Within this ridiculously tiny sample, "the Zoloft was undetectable in 7 of the 11 breastfeeding infants' serum and minimal in the other infants." Multiply that by one hundred, and it could mean detectable levels of Zoloft in 40 out of 110 babies. The amounts may be small, but at least in this speech he doesn't discuss the potential long-term risks of extended exposure to these small amounts in a tiny human.

Dora Kohen, a professor of women's mental health and perinatal psychiatrist, cautions in a 2005 article that "the levels of all antidepressants in exposed infants are not well studied. . . . Research on the subject is limited and most studies do not have the necessary power to support categorical guidelines. . . . The current available research does not allow any absolute and clear recommendation because much of the work on psychotropic medication in breast-feeding is limited to single case reports, small series and naturalistic data collection."[11]

Even the Academy of Breastfeeding Medicine (ABM) worries about the quality of studies currently used to support policy recommendations on antidepressants and breastfeeding. "Despite many publications of antidepressants and breastfeeding, the scientific literature lacks both the breadth and depth for clinicians and mothers to make confident decisions about individual medications," states a report the ABM wrote for the National Guideline Clearinghouse. "The literature suffers from a lack of any randomized clinical trials in lactating women for any class of antidepressant. . . . The majority of studies provide information about the amount of medication detected in breastmilk and maternal serum. Some studies also provide information about infant serum levels of medication. Few studies report infant behavioral outcomes."[12]

When it comes to medications used during pregnancy, the methodologies for determining safety are similarly limited. This is because, due to potential risk to the fetus, randomized, controlled clinical trials would be dangerous and unethical.[13] So if, say, a drug with a chemical profile similar to Aleve is even suspected of possibly affecting the fetus's heart when taken by the mom, the FDA slaps a warning on Aleve, even if there have been no tests on Aleve itself. In the case of psychopharmaceuticals, where the same types of restrictions are levied just as haphazardly, what choice does a woman have? Stay on the drug but not get pregnant because of a potential risk? Or go off the drug, doing harm to her own mental state, in order to protect her fetus from a possibly negligible risk?

It's a crappy choice, and one we unfortunately must make based on very little empirical evidence. But when it comes to how these same drugs conflict with breastfeeding, we do have a viable choice: formula. So why are doctors accused of being anti-breastfeeding for giving the facts (that lactation medicine has not evolved to a point where we can say without a doubt that antidepressants, or pain killers, or what have you, will not affect your baby in a significant way) to nursing moms who are on medication? We have just as much right to know that the studies aren't quite there yet, and to be able to weigh our options, as we do to not be instructed to wean simply because a doctor doesn't know the relative risk. It goes both ways. If the only "acceptable" research comes from breastfeeding advocates, with an inescapable internal bias, then the scales may be tipped too far in one direction. Women will have to make decisions under a thick fog, made up of vague warnings about the "risks of not breastfeeding" versus the risks of relying on minimal scientific evidence. And states of depression or mental duress are not the most conducive to making major decisions, even under the best of circumstances.

• • •

Because of our pediatrician's understandable inability to give me "permission" to treat the depression chemically and keep breastfeeding, I was hesitant to seek professional help. I couldn't pick my own selfish needs over the health of my child. I wouldn't stop breastfeeding just because I was stupid enough to get depressed. As if I didn't feel like a terrible mom already.

A few months after I gave birth, a study published in the aptly titled journal *Medical Hypotheses* claimed that the cessation of breastfeeding simulates child loss. According to the authors, from a biological, anthropological perspective, "the decision to bottle feed unwittingly mimics conditions associated with the death of an infant." And since "child loss is a well documented trigger for depression particularly in mothers," the findings of the study joined the "growing evidence [that] shows that bottle feeding is a risk factor for postpartum depression."[14] The ominous takeaway message rang out over the Internet. "Does bottle feeding cause postpartum depression?" asked one natural parenting website's headline;[15] "Mothers who bottle feed their infants in lieu of breastfeeding put themselves at risk of developing postpartum depression," warned another site, directed at general consumer healthcare.[16]

But two years later, a different study examining the same issues produced markedly different results. Dr. Alison Stuebe, a respected member of the Academy of Breastfeeding Medicine, found that women who reported trouble breastfeeding in the first weeks after giving birth had a 42 percent higher risk of developing postpartum depression than those who enjoyed nursing their babies. Stuebe told *Time* that although it was important to advocate for breastfeeding, clinicians should "look not just at baby's mouth and the boob but to also look at mom's brain" and urged providers to take a more personal approach to infant feeding recommendations: "If, for this mother, and this baby, extracting milk and delivering it to her infant have overshadowed all other aspects of their relationship, it may be that exclusive breast-feeding is not best for them—in fact, it may not even be good for them."[17]

Complicating matters further, unless a woman manages to find a therapist who is out for her best interests and completely aware of up-to-date, current research, she's at risk of falling victim to vague concepts of maternal responsibility, relative risk, and philosophies about holistic care. Plus, it's typically not therapists but pediatricians who are the de facto diagnosticians for postpartum depression—which is a tricky situation, as the moms are not actually their patients. The standard practice for postpartum care in the United States entails a prerelease visit with an obstetrician prior to leaving the hospital (very often not your regular obstetrician, but rather whoever is on call), and a six-week postpartum visit. For women like me who start exhibiting postpartum mood disorder symptoms well before that six-week appointment, this just doesn't cut it. Responsibility for diagnosis and care then falls to pediatricians, who are seeing the mother while examining her newborn a few days after birth, as well as at the child's first well-baby appointment, typically two weeks later. If they are the only medical professionals a new mother comes into contact with, is it their responsibility to provide care or diagnosis to that mother? And are they even qualified to do so?

There is one other "medical professional" that many women encounter in those first weeks, the time period so vital to catching postpartum depression, and that is the lactation consultant. These individuals are sometimes registered nurses, but in order to become an international board-certified lactation consultant (IBCLC)—the "gold standard" for the profession, although the designation is not necessary to work in the lactation counseling field—you do not need a medical degree of any sort. The IBCLC website lists "three pathways" to become eligible for membership; a prospective lactation consultant needs to follow only one of these in order to take the IBCLC exam.[18] Through 2011, only one of these pathways required a "health discipline education" (one semester-long course from an institute of higher learning) in six healthcare-related subjects; for the other two, this rudimentary education was recommended but not required. Beginning in 2012, all three pathways require completion of these courses, but at the time I was consulting with my conga line of lactation consultants, they were in no legal way required to have more medical or psychiatric knowledge than I did. They certainly would have known more about breastfeeding than I—the IBCLC certification does require extensive "lactation specific clinical experience" (from three hundred to one thousand hours, depending on the pathway)—but in terms of recognizing both maternal and infant mental or physical health problems, I'm not sure that, technically, they'd have been any more qualified than anyone with a working knowledge of WebMD.

In a 2005 textbook used for training lactation consultants, the authors discuss the concept of formula-feeding guilt. "Appropriate guilt can be a positive emotion within the realm of personal growth. . . . When you are open and honest with parents regarding the risks of artificial feeding, you will usually find that they appreciate learning what to watch for if they later introduce formula into their baby's diet. You can help parents make guilt work for them as a catalyst to become the best parents they can be."[19] I'm picturing this attitude inflicted on a mother with PPD. Conflict of interest is far too tame a term, but I don't know what else to call it.

It stands to reason that anyone who pursues a career in lactation is going to be pretty passionate about breastfeeding. Even taking the most altruistic view of lactation professionals, how can we expect them to give an unbiased opinion on how breastfeeding might be affecting the mental state of a mother? Much like pediatricians, their professional focus is on something separate from (but thought to be related to) maternal psychology. It's unfair to place the weight of such decisions on the shoulders of someone whose primary purpose is helping women fulfill lactation goals (or, in lesser hands, the lactation consultant's own perception of what constitutes "breastfeeding success").

On the other hand, it's hard to understand why the mother's mental state isn't more integral to breastfeeding-related education and services. In lactation-related literature, the mother and child are often called the "nursing dyad," as if they were one entity. If breastfeeding creates a symbiotic relationship, then the health of the mom is directly related to the baby, as much as the converse. Why would a depressed or suffering mom be considered acceptable?

Back in the 1960s and 1970s, theories on infant "attachment" and the "maternal/infant bond" posited that there was a "critical period" when babies formed either secure or insecure attachments to a primary caregiver—in most cases, for obvious reasons, the mother. Based on the work of John Bowlby, it was thought that a securely attached infant would use his mother as a sort of "home base"; he could explore the world, depending on his mother for comfort and security when things got too intense. If a kid was insecurely attached, the mom-as-safety-net concept didn't hold; an insecurely attached baby would actually avoid physical contact with his mom and take longer to recover from periods of distress.[20]

By the 1980s, most experts had officially dismissed this "attachment theory," especially the idea of a critical period beyond which there is no hope of correcting problems, because the original studies that formed the basis for this theory were flawed.[21] But the ideas behind attachment theory still permeate breastfeeding literature, which is chock-full of references to the "maternal-infant bond" and "attachment." (Ironically, Bowlby himself believed that attachment was formed through the interactions of the primary caregiver and the child, rather than the act of feeding in and of itself, or "individual differences in feeding, such as breast or bottle.")[22]

Later research into attachment discovered that "sensitively and consistently" responding to our infants' cues—cues like crying, smiling, and eye contact—creates that coveted secure attachment; being unresponsive, unpredictable, disengaged, or, on the other end of the spectrum, overly intrusive results in insecure attachment[23] and a hefty bill from the child psychiatrist somewhere down the line. Interestingly, the behaviors blamed for causing insecure attachment not only are related to postpartum depression but could also be attributed to breastfeeding problems. Extreme nipple pain, clogged ducts, or mastitis can cause feedings to be unbearably painful; insufficient milk can be anxiety-provoking. Is it too much of a stretch to suggest that physical pain and anxiety could cause a mom to act "overly intrusive," "unpredictable," or "disengaged"? Sociologist and researcher Stephanie Knaak says that despite numerous claims in parenting literature that breastfeeding leads to better bonding, "It's not going to be the same for all women. For some women, it's not at all about closeness and bonding, because they don't actually enjoy breastfeeding. They don't enjoy the physical aspect of it."[24]

Many of the moms who've written personal stories of breastfeeding failure as part of an ongoing feature on my blog have talked about formula allowing them to "finally be a mom"; all their energy had gone into breastfeeding, a process that often took so much out of them physically and mentally that they had nothing left to give to their babies. "I chose to breastfeed primarily for the opportunity to bond with [my son], although, of course, I also wanted all the health and nutrition benefits," one woman wrote.

> However, this process was starting to feel like anti-bonding. Instead of cuddling with my baby I was fighting with him to get him to latch while he wiggled and squirmed and cried. Instead of caring for my baby's needs, I was hooked up to the pump while my husband took charge of changing him, feeding him, and rocking him to sleep. . . . I didn't want to spend my first weeks and months with my newborn in constant tears, fighting an uphill battle that exhausted all of us and potentially left me feeling resentful and drained. I didn't want my relationship with my son to become about food.[25]

For those of us who have had extreme physical difficulty or emotional discomfort with breastfeeding, formula may allow us to stay calm, connected, and responsive to our children in a way that breastfeeding can't. Some women have also told me that they believed their breastfeeding struggles made them better mothers, leading them to focus more intensely on meeting their babies' needs in other ways. Irvin Leon, of the University of Michigan, argues a similar point regarding the benefits of adoptive parenting:

> Biological parents may be inclined to believe that their genetic connection with their offspring will inevitably solidify the emotional bond with their young. It may feel a bit less important to parent when one is so assured of being the parent. Adoptive parents, not having that genetic connection, must rely on the actual parent-child bond as the principal determinant of parenthood. Attachment theory . . . make[s] it clear that in the eyes of a child the sense of Mommy and Daddy is based on who takes care of that child, meeting that child's needs, and knowing that child's uniqueness and individuality in moment-by-moment daily interactions.[26]

Yet, we are forced to balance our desire to connect and bond with our children in a way that actually works for *us* with what society tells us constitutes bonding. Another guest blogger on my site, a mom of twins, wrote of this worst kind of Catch-22:

> I spent at least a year feeling like the world's worst mother. . . . [M]y depression was focused almost exclusively on my failure to breastfeed. . . . I felt like I should give my babies away to a "real" mother (i.e., one who could produce milk), I felt like I should get pregnant again right away so I could try again to breastfeed, and I contemplated suicide because I was obviously a failure at the most basic level. It didn't help that everywhere I turned I was hit over the head with the "breast is best" message. From the posters in the pediatrician's office to the message on the side of each formula can, I couldn't escape it.[27]

In a review of breastfeeding's impact on the mother-infant relationship, Norwegian behavioral scientists found that out of forty-one papers discussing breastfeeding and the maternal bond, twenty-two of them made "general statements on the positive effect of breastfeeding on either facet of the mother-infant relationship without a reference to empirical studies supporting this claim."[28] The study authors then examined the papers which did provide evidence backing these claims, and came to the conclusion that "breastfeeding may promote the maternal bond, *but mothers who bond better with their infants may also be more likely to choose to breastfeed* over bottle-feeding." (Emphasis mine.) Think about it—a mother who is already nervous, depressed, or stressed may have a tougher time bonding with a newborn. This mother may ultimately turn to bottle feeding to control at least one aspect of her new, overwhelming life. Or consider how a baby having trouble feeding may act on a daily basis. A hungry, frustrated baby does not a happy baby make (or a happy mother, for that matter). In both cases, the maternal bond may be affected and bottles may replace breastfeeding. So although it is true that the mothers of these bottle-feeding babies may exhibit less positive, "bonded" behavior toward their children, is it the fault of the bottle? Or was it the situation that led the mom to the bottle that also caused difficulty bonding?

The same question holds for the connection between breastfeeding and postpartum depression. Like the studies mentioned earlier in this chapter, some researchers have found a correlation between lack of breastfeeding and higher incidence of depression; however, the majority of these studies don't factor in why the mother isn't breastfeeding in the first place. A 2009 study found that women who exhibited pregnancy-related anxiety or prenatal depressive symptoms were roughly two times more likely than women without these mood disorders to plan to formula feed.[29] "Prenatal mood disorders may affect a woman's plans to breastfeed and may be early risk factors for failure to breastfeed," the researchers point out. Even if the intention to breastfeed is there, multiple factors inform infant-feeding choices once a woman leaves the hospital. Feeling like a failure, dealing with pain, frustration, and exhaustion, and having a baby who screams at the sight of her, could make any mother feel overwhelmed, let alone one who's already on the brink of actual PPD. Maybe for those of us more prone to anxiety or depression, the stress of breastfeeding struggles is just the camel's dreaded straw.

• • •

Back in fifth grade, the most popular girl in our class, Caroline McCloskey, utilized the new invention of consumer telephone conference-calling in a creative way: she'd get you on the line, call another girl, and get her to talk about you (assumedly) behind your back, while you silently listened in. This was cruel to both the person talking crap and the person being talked about; still, there was a strange thrill in hearing what someone actually said about you when they thought you weren't listening. Reading the transcripts of breastfeeding conferences feels remarkably similar to this childhood game. Discovering what people (including some of the most respected figures in breastfeeding advocacy) actually think about formula-feeding mothers is devastating but also validates what most bottle feeders suspect: there is shockingly little understanding of the lived reality of breastfeeding "failure." For example, during a panel at the annual Symposium on Breastfeeding and Feminism at the University of North Carolina, Schatzi H. McCarthy voiced some strong opinions about why women do not nurse: "The reality is that many women in America choose not to breastfeed because of: 1) pain or discomfort (often cited as 'breastfeeding difficulty' in the literature); and 2) the raw sexuality of the breast and its existence as an object of attraction for the male—likewise, the need to keep it looking its best. . . . When we erroneously believe that the health and vitality of our young is not easily compromised through the usage of infant formulas . . . the logic follows that we should use them—to avoid sacrificing our own comfort and our youth."[30]

I can only cite the people who frequent my blog as evidence, but I have yet to meet a woman who isn't breastfeeding because she doesn't want to "sacrifice her own comfort and youth." The refusal to acknowledge the legitimacy of personal reasons for not breastfeeding could be written off as a misunderstanding; the experience of motherhood is a tough thing to measure and varies depending on socioeconomic, ethnic, and geographical factors. You can't really look at a study of immigrant communities in Arizona and compare that to the experience of an upper

Westside Manhattanite, and yet this is in effect what advocacy groups try to do. It may indeed be true that for some women in bottle-feeding cultures like the American southeastern seaboard, bottle feeding is motivated by a pervading fear of drooping breasts. But that is not the only reason women choose not to breastfeed.

Since I felt I had gone to "appropriate" lengths trying to nurse, when I began writing as the Fearless Formula Feeder I still harbored a suspicion that most women who formula fed from the beginning were doing so for "practical" reasons, which some might even consider selfish. I didn't think there was anything wrong with that; after what I'd been through, I wouldn't blame anyone for choosing the path of least resistance. But I assumed these choices were made for the reasons put forth by advocacy literature: convenience, desire to get one's body back, an unsupportive environment. This all changed the day I received an email from K.

K had been a frequent poster on Fearless Formula Feeder for months before she wrote to me explaining her real reasons for formula feeding. "I was 14 when I was raped," she began.

> I come from a place where breastfeeding rates are high. It's the normal, responsible and practical thing to do. When I thought about having babies in the future, I imagined holding that child in my arms and breastfeeding it. . . . I felt that way right up until about the 6 month mark of my first pregnancy. At first it started out with feelings of dread. A person, *using* my body again. . . . I started waking at 2 am in sweat after nightmares of a baby suckling blood from me; having panic attacks and breaking down in tears. . . . I started to *hate* the baby growing inside me. . . . I hated the fact I would be made to feed this thing from my breasts, my most sensitive part of my body, that had had so much damage done to them in the past. . . . I felt I couldn't discuss it with anyone because I got the "it will be fine" talk

> or looked down at for feeling this way about my baby. . . . I couldn't even discuss it with my partner or my best friend. . . . I felt so ashamed, so guilty.

When I posted K's story on my blog, I began receiving emails from other women who had similar experiences. One wrote to say that she'd been totally unprepared for how her past sexual trauma could affect her first breastfeeding experience. "I was shocked to find . . . that it creeped me out. Badly. I was not prepared for the first of several flashbacks that would come that day. I felt horror at my perceived perpetuation of the cycle of abuse upon my newborn son. Good Lord, I just shoved my boob in his mouth! He was crying! What had I just done? Each time he was put to breast, I wanted to fling him across the room. I would close my eyes and cry while the hospital LC tried to get him to latch."

"I was 17 when I was raped by a boyfriend," wrote another woman in the comment section of K's guest post. "And no one knows, not my husband or my mom or my best friend, which is why I'm leaving this comment anonymously instead of signing in. . . . This is EXACTLY why it makes me so angry when people say 'all women should at least try to breastfeed.' You never know what someone has been through and it would be cruel to expect someone to explain WHY she chose to not even try."

I uphold a pretty lenient comment policy, but sometimes I regret my stance on censorship; seeing the next comment left on K's post was one of those times. "That's an awful story, but have you ever heard of counseling? Sheesh," the anonymous contributor wrote. "I can't believe that your midwife, a health professional, didn't refer you for mental health services AND tell you the truth about the risks of artificial feeding to your baby. Healthcare fail." So much for the milk of human kindness.

• • •

It's not only survivors of sexual trauma who have been left out of the breastfeeding discourse. While infant feeding experts have debated the cause/effect of depression on breastfeeding, they've barely touched the surface of how other psychological or emotional problems might factor in to a woman's "failure" to breastfeed. Some of these conditions, like sensory disorders that make bodily contact unbearable, are relatively rare; public health discourse must focus on the population level, so a condition that affects only a statistically insignificant number of women can understandably be dismissed. But when one in five women suffers from some type of eating disorder,[31] you're talking about an *incredibly* significant number of mothers. Body image and weight issues are barely acknowledged in the popular breastfeeding literature, unless it's a dismissive shout-out to vanity (most articles on the "myths" of breastfeeding assure women that nursing won't ruin their breasts, as if this were a primary reason for choosing formula).

One 1996 study on body image and breastfeeding found that women intending to nurse had higher levels of satisfaction with their body shape.[32] Other studies have suggested that breastfeeding can enhance self-esteem and even give women with eating disorders a brief respite from symptoms (although these same studies admit that once weaning has commenced, the troublesome behaviors come back with a vengeance). But what about when breastfeeding exacerbates symptoms? Having swollen, enormous, leaking breasts was not just physically uncomfortable for me; it brought back every dark thought, every weird insecurity from a ten-year struggle with anorexia. I hated that the issues of my youth were still plaguing me in my thirties, and especially that they were infringing on my ability to care for my child. But I couldn't help feeling disgusted every time I looked down at my chest.

"Concerns about body image . . . tend to be overlooked in the moral hierarchy of motivational factors influencing women's infant-feeding decisions [but] were significant factors in participants' decisions to both formula feed and breastfeed their infants," write Stapleton and colleagues in their 2008 study examining the connection between eating disorders and infant feeding.[33]

The authors state that "a desire to . . . resume regimes which had previously been employed to control and shape the body, was a significant motivator" for choosing not to breastfeed. One could feasibly still breastfeed while starving oneself or engaging in bingeing and purging—after all, if starving women in third-world countries are able to make sufficient milk, why couldn't an anorexic—but at what emotional cost? According to Stapleton and colleagues, "for eating disordered women who are already exceedingly image-conscious, but who generally project a negative body image, it is suggested that the prospect of breastfeeding may stimulate uncomfortable, and unmanageable, feelings about identity and experience."[34]

Some of the women in the Stapleton study chose to breastfeed because they believed it would help them lose the pregnancy weight. This tends to be a strong motivational factor in studies examining women's reasons for breastfeeding; it may not be politically correct to admit that you're nursing for "selfish" reasons, but burning an extra five hundred calories a day sounds awfully appealing when you're desperate to fit back into your favorite jeans. "The 'selfish' drive to recover the pre-pregnant [eating disordered] figure seemed to be at least as powerful a motivator for women to breastfeed as were altruistic desires to privilege the welfare of the baby," write the authors. But they also warn that "breastfeeding is not necessarily synonymous with maternal weight loss and indeed one prominent researcher in the field reports that 'there is surprisingly little evidence that breastfeeding makes women lose more weight after pregnancy.'" For a woman with an eating disorder, the reality of breastfeeding's ability to expedite postpartum weight loss, compared to what the popular mythology has promised, can feel like the ultimate betrayal, and several women in the study "stated that they would have ceased breastfeeding much earlier in order to resume their binge/purge activities had they known that weight loss did not automatically follow from breastfeeding."[35]

It may be hard for someone without an eating disorder to understand just how difficult breastfeeding can be for someone afflicted with this condition. I think we've all watched enough daytime talk shows to know that eating disorders are not simply about being skinny; they are undeniably linked with a need for control. Nursing—hell, motherhood in general—is all about letting go of control. Especially at the beginning, when your baby needs to eat, you need to make your breast available. Skip a feeding and your boobs will make you pay for it—some of my bras are still stained with wasted milk from days that I didn't make it to the pump in time. Your breasts are bigger, fuller, and the nipples . . . well, they don't look like they used to. I expect for most women, this is a small and insignificant price to pay for the incredible gift of being able to singlehandedly nourish your child (also, the enhanced cleavage may very well be a positive thing for those who haven't spent their lives wishing for smaller breasts).

For me, however, this literal full-ness was stifling. The physical sensation of let-down—a tingling, burning heaviness—rooted me in my body; I had spent years trying to float above my corporeal self as a coping mechanism, and this felt like hell. I hadn't lost any of my pregnancy weight and, with the larger breasts, I felt even bigger than I had during my third trimester. Every time I opened my shirt and was forced to look at my naked torso, I wanted to scream. For those of us with eating disorders, feelings about physicality go far beyond appearances. It's a pain you can taste, an inability to escape from what feels like a ponderous weight. It's a prison, one that I'd finally escaped five years earlier, and managed to avoid for nine precarious months of steady weight gain. But here I was, locked up again, and the only means of escape would mean forever damning myself to the labels *selfish, vain,* and *weak.*

That wasn't an option, so I chose to take Zoloft and risk the consequences. Within days of starting back on antidepressants, my mind started to sharpen. I could look at Leo without shaking. But although drugs may have enhanced my serotonin levels, they couldn't stop my child from screaming in fear every time I pulled down my shirt; they couldn't pump my milk for me, allowing me the rest I needed to truly heal or the time I wanted to begin bonding with my baby, to start feeling like an actual mother rather than a milk depository. At least the drugs gave me the strength to keep going, despite the anxiety that each feeding time provoked, as I waited as patiently as I could for that legendary bond to happen. And eventually, it did—albeit with a three-hundred-dollar breast pump.

FOUR

The Dairy Queens

American mothers are stuck between a rock and a hard place—or, more accurately, a breast and a breast pump. In millennial America, most women are going back to work within a few months of giving birth;[1] in order to feed their children breastmilk exclusively for the recommended six months, some of that milk is not going to be straight from the tap. This has meant that breastfeeding has come to mean primarily breast*pumping* for a large group of mothers,[2] and breastfeeding rights have been superseded by the need for "lactation-friendly" workplaces that allow for adequate expression of milk. Feminist discussion of breastfeeding has been lodged between this same rock and hard place, focusing mostly on surface workplace breastfeeding issues and all but ignoring the potential danger that breastfeeding advocacy might essentialize women down to biological functions.

The trouble is that there are fundamental differences—both philosophically and biologically—between breastfeeding and serving pumped milk in a bottle. As defined by WHO, the term *exclusive breastfeeding* means no bottles, regardless of what's in them.[3] The skin-to-skin emotional closeness of breastfeeding is nullified when you're bonding with a machine rather than your child; babies fed from a bottle, no matter what its contents, are supposedly prone to issues with intake regulation, potentially putting them at risk for later obesity;[4] and even certain components of the milk itself are altered in the process of pumping, storage, and delivery. Studies show that antioxidant activity is greatly decreased in both refrigerated and frozen breastmilk as compared to fresh (the authors of one study recommend using all pumped milk within forty-eight hours,[5] which puts a damper on the common maternity leave practice of creating a "freezer stash" in preparation for going back to work); cellular activity and vitamins B_6 and C are also reduced, as are some of the immunological properties.[6] Since historically, breastfeeding studies haven't been great about defining exactly what "breastfeeding" means, we don't know if the benefits are as bountiful for those kids who are bottle-fed pumped milk as for those who are completely *breast*fed.

Having women express their milk also creates a commercial market that undermines the claim that breastfeeding is "free." After the frenulectomy and several more visits with lactation consultants, it became clear that Leo was probably not going to latch successfully in the immediate future; we finally decided I would pump all of his food and serve it to him in the bottles he so loved, while still attempting to put him to the breast whenever possible (I followed this plan for exactly a week, before exhaustion and pessimism got the best of me, at which point I gratefully accepted the label of "exclusive pumper"). The moderately priced single pump we'd originally purchased had seemed sufficient when we thought I'd be pumping only supplementally, but once we'd made this decision, it became abundantly clear that we needed to step it up a notch. In consumer terms, I was in the same market as working moms—women who needed a high-functioning machine that would extract the most milk in the shortest amount of time. The Mercedes of pumps was the Medela Pump-in-Style, marketed to working moms as offering "portable convenience for quiet, discreet pumping anywhere" in "an attractive microfiber tote for fast and easy pumping" with the ability to pump "more milk in less time" and "keep the connection to your baby even when you're not there."[7] Considering the price tag of this apparatus (as of this writing, it retails for a hefty $279 at Target), it's wise that they market it mainly to professionals, because you'll need a second salary to afford the darn thing. My pumping days were a couple of years too early for a 2011 tax law that legitimized breastfeeding costs as a medical expense;[8] at the time, some insurance companies were starting to cover or subsidize the cost of a pump, but our insurance company apparently hadn't gotten the progressively-pro-breastfeeding memo. We ended up renting a hospital-grade double pump, at the modest price of sixty-five dollars per month, from a hospital about forty minutes away. The drive was worth it; our own hospital charged upward of eighty dollars per month to rent the same equipment.

The cost, commercialism, and reality of pumping conflicts with the way breastfeeding is typically promoted, causing consternation for those fighting to raise breastfeeding rates.

But the reality is that in order to avoid formula, most working women will have to pump significant amounts of milk—and accordingly, breastfeeding advocates need to ensure that employers cooperate. The Breastfeeding Promotion Act, introduced by Rep. Carolyn Maloney (D–New York) to Congress in June 2009, was designed to create tax incentives for employers that "encourage" their female employees to breastfeed and provide pumping facilities at work. Although giving pumping moms an easier time is a great idea, the language used in the discussion of this act is troubling. Maloney's literature uses the argument that not breastfeeding is a public health threat, listing the requisite statistics about reduction of disease,[9] even though few studies have controlled for whether the babies categorized as "breastfed" were cared for at home (like the majority of truly exclusively breastfed babies would need to be) or in germ-ridden daycare centers. The rhetoric invoked to argue for better pumping rights leans heavily on the claim that more breastfeeding leads to less employee absenteeism due to sick kids, but this claim rests on shaky ground, as Mary C. Noonan, assistant professor of sociology at the University of Iowa, and Phyllis L. F. Rippeyoung, assistant professor and coordinator of women's and gender studies at Acadia University, found when studying the economic impact of breastfeeding.

> Breastfeeding advocates point to research that finds formula-fed infants are more likely to be sick than breastfed infants and so breastfeeding employees may miss less work to care for sick children than formula-feeding employees. . . . If this is the case, women who choose to breastfeed may actually be more likely to work and/or work more hours because their children are healthier and thus less of a barrier to productive participation in the labor force. Research by Cohen, Mrtek, and Mrtek (1995) is the most often cited research on this issue. This study is based on a small sample of women and finds that formula fed infants are more likely to be sick than breastfed infants. However, the modal number of missed days of work due to a sick child is zero for both groups *and only 3 percent more*

formula feeding mothers than breastfeeding mothers missed more than one day of work due to a sick infant.[10] (Emphasis mine.)

Considering this, and considering that WHO makes a point of designating pumped milk as the "second best choice" for infant nutrition (the first being breastmilk direct from the breast),[11] wouldn't we be better off fighting for longer maternity leaves, giving women the opportunity to stay home and nurse their babies? Or, alternatively, advocating for on-site daycare centers so that working women could breastfeed their children during the workday (a practice that has, incidentally, been shown to increase the chance of breastfeeding past the six-month mark by a whopping 59 percent),[12] so that "breastfeeding does not have to become a disembodied practice involving machines and bottles"?[13]

It's odd that these pumping policies are considered "family-friendly," when they have little to do with easing the burden of women juggling what sociologist Arlie Hochschild dubbed the "second shift" (implying that working moms have to balance paid work with a myriad of responsibilities at home).[14] Instead, all the focus on pumping, and the advocacy tools used to ensure that women can pump successfully, just adds to the stress of the working mother. Sociologist and Fordham University professor Orit Avishai has argued that "accommodations for breast-feeding women who pump their breasts in their place of employment [can] exacerbate, rather than alleviate, women's double burdens." In her 2002 article "Family-Friendly as a Double-Edged Sword," Avishai reports on in-depth interviews she conducted with first-time, middle-class mothers in the breastfeeding-friendly San Francisco Bay Area, attempting to discover exactly how lactation-friendly policies affected these women.[15] She chose to focus on educated, professional women, since breastfeeding rates are highest among this group—and, more important, because these are the women who have work situations most conducive to pumping. Although recent government activity has made lactation-friendly workplaces a more widespread phenomenon, it stands to reason that women who are salaried, held in high value by their organizations, and have more control over time and office real estate (i.e., a private office) are going to have the most ideal pumping scenarios; if these women are experiencing difficulty with the process, then that says a lot. And for the women in Avishai's study, having "difficulty" is putting it mildly.

"One thing that really came out when I was doing a lot of interviews with women was that I'd ask, how do you [manage breastfeeding and pumping]? What's involved? And they would launch into these twenty-minute narratives about all the work that goes into it," Avishai tells me via phone one summer afternoon, eight years after this paper was published. "And then they start talking about, you know, I bought this, that, and the other; or they have all these stories about what they set up and how long it takes to get into it. . . . And for that group who had autonomy, who had control over time and space for the most part . . . it was incredibly difficult to keep up long-term. Some were very successful, others not so, but the general story was, it's hard. It's hard to do."[16]

Even the logistics of getting the milk pumped in the first place are complicated, a multistep process Avishai details in her paper that entails setting up the pump; closing curtains and doors; partially undressing; waiting for the body to cooperate and "let down," which can be difficult in times of stress ("times of stress" being the status quo for women in certain professions—it's hard to relax enough for milk to flow in the middle of a deposition or after a meeting about lackluster quarterly sales); and finally, cleaning the equipment and storing the milk.

Avishai points out that due to this extensive process, "pumping cut heavily into the workday. To ensure maximum results and to avoid painful engorgements as well as embarrassing leaks . . . women arranged their workday around their pumping routines."[17] Even for those with "great work situations" (as one interviewee described her ability to take two fifteen-minute breaks and an hour lunch break every day), this can be difficult to achieve. Several of the mothers Avishai interviewed mentioned that the additional break time needed to pump sufficiently—meaning producing enough milk to completely meet their babies' needs, as feeding exclusively breastmilk for a year was the common goal—resulted in extended work hours (trying to make up for lost time) and longer days in general. Avishai quotes a message board thread she followed in which participants encouraged a pumping mom to add pumping sessions overnight and in the wee hours of the morning, when milk production was the highest; I can only imagine how a mother who is working all day, coming home to spend time with her child, dealing with an infant waking numerous times during the night, and trying to spend five minutes connecting with her spouse finds the energy to sacrifice sleep for pumping sessions, without going completely batty.

As part of the Obama administration's health care reform, a 2010 amendment to the Fair Labor Standards Act (FLSA) made it law that employers allow "reasonable break time" and "a place, other than a bathroom, that is shielded from view and free from intrusion from coworkers and the public" where a woman can express breastmilk, for one year after the child's birth.[18] There are several caveats to this, though: if your company has fewer than fifty employees, the rules don't apply and you better not expect to be paid for these pumping breaks. Plus, "reasonable break time" is not clearly defined; the literature from the U.S. Department of Labor just states that "the frequency of breaks needed to express breast milk as well as the duration of each break will likely vary." In the early months of 2011, First Lady Michelle Obama publicly encouraged women to breastfeed, as part of her anti-obesity campaign.[19] But despite the new provisions that came with her husband's health care reform, exclusive breastfeeding while working full-time is a lot to ask of women—especially those in the lower-paid, lower-status jobs typical of those in the same demographics that suffer from the highest obesity rates. A study from the Institute of Women's Policy Research (IWPR) argues that these provisions will affect mostly lower-status, waged workers, as these were the women who were most likely not given access to breaks or a proper place to pump in the past.[20] Using this logic, we are essentially giving lower-status workers the same lactation rights as higher-status workers—*and higher-status women are still having difficulty pumping at work.* The IWPR study estimates that the new laws will have a significant impact on breastfeeding rates, but the reality remains to be seen—as does the effect these changes will have on women in the workforce.

Rippeyoung and Noonan point out that even if we accept that formula-feeding parents do miss slightly more work due to sick kids, the time required for pumping carries its own potential for lost wages and work time. They estimated that if women spent a combined average of one hour pumping at work per day, over the course of the recommended twenty-four weeks of breastfeeding, "this would equal 120 hours of lost work time due to breastfeeding. Assuming an 8 hour workday, that translates into 15 missed workdays. Even compensating breastfeeding women with one less sick day than their non-breastfeeding counterparts are faced with on average . . . breastfeeding women would lose the equivalent of 14 workdays during their child's first 6 months of life," they write.[21]

In light of these findings, my original question—why aren't we focusing more on extending maternity leaves?—opens up a can of particularly nasty worms. If lobbyists are arguing for longer paid leave in order to reach breastfeeding goals, they need to convince businesses that there will be an economic and/or public health incentive. When a group of economists looked at the effect of a change in Canadian parental leave policies (chiefly, the "large increase in maternity leave entitlements"), their assessment of the effectiveness of these incentives was ambivalent. Although mothers spent more time away from work and duration of breastfeeding increased, the economists found "little effect of the increase in breastfeeding (and parental care) on self-reported indicators of the mother and child (in the first 24 months) health."[22]

This type of research is seldom brought to public attention when discussing workplace lactation rights. It might diminish employer and government support for breastfeeding initiatives, so it's understandable that these findings aren't being shouted from the rooftops. Then again, if we must frame our need for more family-friendly workplace policies in terms of the advantages for our employers, what does that say about how our society values parenthood?

Of course, there's always the option for women to "opt out," to choose motherhood over work, and this is as valid a choice as any—as long as it is a choice made free of subtle coercions and misleading fear tactics. But we also need to remember that not everyone has this choice. "Most of the women who are dropping out [of the workforce] are wealthier women, highly educated women, married to higher earning spouses so they can take time off to breastfeed—it seems to be a very class-based decision," says Mary Noonan. When she and Rippeyoung presented their paper at a conference about feminism and breastfeeding, "some people were saying, well, women should be able to stay home full time and breastfeed. And I just felt like, what planet are you on? Where are they getting the money to pay their rent? A lot of women aren't married, do not have another source of income. It seemed like this pie in the sky idea of what motherhood is all about."[23]

Obviously, if all women were given six months' paid maternity leave, they would have a way to pay their rent and still breastfeed exclusively. But that isn't the reality in present-day America—and even if it were, that doesn't negate the fact that there are other factors that play into a woman's decision to combine breastfeeding and employment. According to Avishai, "The thing I think that gets lost is the fact that, you know, we're not hunter-gatherers anymore, and we don't live in caves. . . . [W]e've got to keep in mind the context in which breastfeeding is happening for women now. So, you've got to redefine 'natural' within the context. And take into account the modern-day pressures."[24]

Rippeyoung and Noonan warn that one of these "modern-day pressures" may lead women to sacrifice professional goals solely for the sake of infant nutrition. "The desire for the health benefits of breastfeeding or the shame felt for not breastfeeding . . . may lead employed mothers who are unable to combine breastfeeding and paid work to opt for breastfeeding in place of paid work, when they are financially able to do so," they write.[25] And for those who don't opt out, combining work with longer breastfeeding (even just a year of nursing, as the AAP and WHO recommend) may have a very real impact on professional prospects. Although the concept of a "motherhood penalty"—the wage penalty women with children experience in comparison to childless women[26]—is nothing new, Mary Noonan describes the results of her research (that women who breastfeed longer earn less money than those who don't) as "the motherhood penalty with an asterisk next to it." This matters, she says, because "breastfeeding may be correlated with better health outcomes, but money is too—so whether or not to breastfeed is not such an obvious decision to make."

In a dissertation examining various factors affecting breastfeeding rates, scholar Alison Jacknowitz cautions that welfare programs that encourage new moms to seek employment may have a deleterious effect, at least in one specific regard: "Holding a job increases the costs of breastfeeding, which in turn could reduce the propensity of new mothers to breastfeed their children. . . . [W]orking negatively affects breastfeeding. . . . [W]hile the primary intention of welfare work requirements is to increase self-sufficiency among impoverished mothers . . . [o]ur results suggest that these policies could impose a significant cost on infants and their mothers by reducing the prevalence of breastfeeding. This cost must be weighed against the potential benefits associated with the rise in employment."[27] The success of welfare-to-work programs is debatable for a myriad of other reasons, but it seems a bit Orwellian to argue against a program that could theoretically empower mothers, affording them self-esteem and self-sufficiency, in order to raise breastfeeding rates.

Despite what the government and breastfeeding advocates are so admirably trying to accomplish by encouraging "lactation-friendly" workplaces, it's not an obvious decision to exclusively breastfeed while working full-time, even if you are allotted several breaks and don't have to pump in a restroom. There are human factors that complicate things further. Women attempting to combine breastfeeding and paid work are left dangling in a nebulous space; much of the pro-breastfeeding discourse is wrapped up in a biologic-essentialist view of gender, with the assumption that child-rearing should come before work for women, that the professional world should accommodate us, and if it can't, then it's our responsibility to choose the welfare of our kids over professional or financial gain. I think most moms would agree that their kids are more important than their jobs, but it's not always financially feasible for a mother to forgo employment. For other women, being professionally fulfilled is integral to self-worth—which brings things right back to the dead-end argument that a happy, healthy mom makes for a happy and healthy baby.

Even the working women who believe deeply in breastfeeding may find themselves in a bind, at a loss for emotional support. La Leche League is the most readily available outlet for breastfeeding support, but the organization has a spotty history in its interactions with employed mothers. I spoke with Christina Bobel, a professor of women's studies at the University of Massachusetts and the author of *The Paradox of Natural Mothering,* who spent time getting to know La Leche League from a personal and professional perspective. She stressed that although individual chapters may vary, in the official League literature the topic of working women is approached very tentatively. "I think it crystallizes around pumping," she mused.

> I mean, I think there is this almost shrouded discomfort with working outside the home while nursing because of how it complicates breastfeeding. As a mother who worked and breastfed and pumped, I get that. It's complicated. And I think to say, "it will

> be no problem, just go ahead and breastfeed" ... well, I think it's just disingenuous and actually quite damaging for League or anyone to say that, because then women will begin blaming themselves when things aren't working out. [But] I also think that League's approach of touting a line of support for working mothers, and then not providing the practical tools to make it work, is also destructive.[28]

Bobel gives an example of a woman asking about a workplace breastfeeding issue, who, rather than getting practical advice, was told that maybe she shouldn't be working. "That's not helpful at all. She was looking for really concrete advice," she says, and suggests that this lack of support may stem from ignorance more than from denigration.

> What often happens is that the League leaders themselves often do not work outside the home while breastfeeding small children, so they've never experienced it. They don't know what it's like to try to pump while you've got somebody knocking on the storeroom door. Or the terror and the panic of the night before. . . . I remember thinking, it's Tuesday night, I have to pump enough for daycare on Wednesday, and it's not working ... and now I'm going to fight with my partner, the baby's screaming, I want to hold her [instead of pumping] my breasts, and I'm panicked. And so I'm saying to my partner, "I think we have to go buy formula because we don't have any breastmilk for tomorrow." It was terrorizing. I felt like a failure, I was distraught, feeling guilty about my decision to put her in daycare.[29]

Linda Blum, author of *At the Breast: Ideologies of Breastfeeding and Motherhood in the Contemporary United States,* believes that despite all the talk about breastfeeding and raising breastfeeding rates, we are actually just talking about "women pumping and using the bottle." "We're not even talking about the physical experience of being with your baby anymore," she says. "When some authors speak of what an empowering, incredible experience breastfeeding is and lament that feminists like me do not embrace it, I think they are ignoring the reality of the breast pump. I *did* talk to women about pumping, and no one's finding it very empowering, and no one's finding it body-affirming."[30]

When I was pumping exclusively for Leo, I had to excuse myself to express my milk every two hours. Friends and family would shift uncomfortably in their seats, as if I'd just announced I had to change a tampon, as if pumping was something private and embarrassing. I couldn't really blame them. The reaction had been different in the first week when I excused myself to *nurse* Leo; breastfeeding was something sacred and sweet (even if they didn't want to see me do it—but I think they were trying to respect my privacy, rather than feeling disgusted by the act or anything similarly insidious). There's a lot of discussion in society about a woman's comfort and rights when nursing in public, but I've yet to see anyone pump in public. And who would want to? I've never seen a pump that didn't resemble a medieval torture device, at least once it was in use. You can dress it up in purple and give it a snazzy carrying case, but you can't disguise the intimidating tubing, slurping suction cups, and whir of the motor. It's a piece of machinery, evocative of mass farming practices, like something out of a PETA film on the unfair treatment of bovines.

My father-in-law caught on to this comparison straight away. Attempting levity, he'd joke about my being the "Dairy Queen," a title I grew to love. It helped to have a sense of humor about these things, because it *was* kind of ridiculous. In order to provide my child with something so inherently "natural," I was more intimately acquainted with technology than I'd ever been before.

I spoke to a slew of fellow Dairy Queens who had pumped at work, asking them to tell me about their experiences. The challenges they faced suggest that the current laws protecting pumping in the workplace aren't going to cut it if we are going to encourage women to lactate on the job. Erin, a teacher who was attempting to pump for her twins, admitted that while the room she was given to pump wasn't completely private (the door had a window, so she had to make sure to sit where no one could see her through the glass), this was the least of her worries.

> The privacy issue pales in comparison to how awful I've been made to feel for pumping at work. My principal is not at all supportive of my choice to pump. She frequently schedules meetings that I have to attend during lunch. Since I'm a teacher, the break between our morning and afternoon sessions is the only time I can pump; I can't meet with parents or other professionals while I'm pumping. When I bring this up, she treats me as if I'm saying I don't want to work. She doesn't seem to understand that I can't just not pump whenever she wants me to do something else. I'm convinced that my need to pump has made her think that I'm a poor employee, when, in actuality, I'm a very hard worker and dedicated to my job. Unfortunately, most of our conversations start with her asking me to do something, and end with me saying that I need to pump. It has made going back to work just miserable for me, and I'm ready to just give up on the whole thing. Pumping already sucks. I don't need my job to make it suck more.

Tracy, who worked as the education director of an aquarium, "had to pump in a public restroom on a dirty chair that people often use to change their children's diapers on. They erected a curtain but my knees were three inches away from the curtain and crowds of children were often just inches away on the other side. I was peeked at by everyone from young toddlers to seven-year-old boys to adults. It was awful," she explains. And while she was technically allowed to pump when she needed, "often I had to skip or be late for a session due to a meeting." Tracy's employer wasn't necessarily doing anything illegal; the FLSA amendment does not specify whether the "place, other than a bathroom, that is shielded from view and free from intrusion from coworkers and the public" has a *door.* Having grade schoolers spy on you does probably qualify as "intrusion from coworkers and the public," but Tracy would have had to take up the case with HR; she already feared for her livelihood and didn't want to rock the boat. "My husband had lost his job, and I felt my job was threatened from the moment I returned from maternity leave."

Unfortunately, no amount of legislation can control how employers feel about a pumping employee; there may be laws protecting that employee's job and rights, but there are subtle ways that coworkers and supervisors can make a breastfeeding mother feel ostracized. Breastfeeding advocates argue that we just need to change the culture we live in; if breastfeeding were the norm, then no one would give pumping professionals flak. Women *should* have the right to combine breastfeeding with work, and in some ways, whatever means we use to secure that end are justified. But until this happens—a process that could easily take a generation or two—working mothers are going to bear the burden of Noonan's motherhood-penalty-plus-asterisk, and not just financially. This is fine if pumping is something they want to do. But when mothers are made to feel as though it's something they *have* to do in order to protect their children from harm, it's a whole other story.

• • •

Feminism and breastfeeding have a highly dysfunctional relationship. According to the World Alliance for Breastfeeding Action (WABA), "Breastfeeding confirms a woman's power to control her own body, and challenges the male-dominated medical model and business interests that promote bottle feeding."[31] But most prominent feminist voices—aside from cautiously mentioning in scholarly journals that breastfeeding may be too sex-specific to support the goal of gender-neutral childbearing—have been conspicuously absent from the debate. The mission statement of the National Organization for Women (NOW), the largest organization of feminist activists in the United States, claims that one of its goals is to "secure abortion, birth control and reproductive rights for all women";[32] it would seem that breastfeeding would fall into the category of "reproductive rights," which would mean NOW should have some official position on breastfeeding. It's not that simple. First off, breastfeeding is not unilaterally accepted as a "reproductive right." According to feminist scholar Judith Galtry, this has much to do with the concept of the "bright line"—basically, that a line needs to be drawn between "female-specific functions" like pregnancy and birth, and the actual child*rearing,* which has the ability to be something either a man or woman can handle.[33]

This distinction has been a source of contention in feminist circles; on the one hand, it could provide fodder to those who don't want to accommodate nursing moms in the workplace; on the other hand, placing breastfeeding on the other side of that bright line further illuminates gender differences and could potentially harm the ability of women to excel in the workplace. Putting the emphasis on breastfeeding as the reason for longer maternity leaves (and having it be maternity leave in the first place, rather than gender-neutral parental leave) does essentialize women to a significant degree.

Things get even more muddled when feminist-related breastfeeding advocacy turns the argument from one of protecting the rights of those who want to breastfeed, to one of biological imperative or social responsibility. Katherine A. Dettwyler, a lactivist and anthropologist most famous for her claim that the "normal" weaning age for modern humans is somewhere between two-and-a-half and seven years old, wrote a strongly worded essay on feminism and breastfeeding, which she posted on her Facebook page in 2009. In it, she accuses mainstream feminists of a myriad of evils that have undermined breastfeeding advocacy efforts. She claims that people have portrayed her as antifeminist for promoting the concept that "breastfeeding has consequences for the health of mothers and children [which] has been portrayed as 'essentializing' women, reducing them to their biological functions, and as a call for a return to a patriarchal, pre-feminist system where women devoted all their time to child-bearing and child-rearing."[34]

Dettwyler does not see her point of view as antifeminist, and spends the rest of the essay explaining why. Yet she speaks of the results of second-wave feminism with derision:

> Which is more important, reproductive success or productive success? . . . The compromise that many modern Western women have settled for is to have only a few children, and to turn much of the care of those children, including bottle feeding, over to others. Some women have chosen to adopt children, rather than go through pregnancy and childbirth themselves, in order to reduce the amount of time and effort they must take away from their jobs. . . . Others do give birth to their own biological children, but insist that childrearing is not their primary focus, and that breastfeeding and other activities that require mother-infant contact are luxuries they can't afford.[35]

The underlying anger and defensiveness in this piece underscores the nature of feminist discourse in this country, especially around issues of motherhood. Feminist scholar H. E. Baber writes that liberal feminists "are not in the business of assessing the 'value' of persons whatever that might come to. . . . [W]omen want a variety of things and different women want different things. . . . [S]ex roles, and conventional expectations about women's behavior, aptitudes and goals, restrict women's options and so undermine preference satisfaction."[36] If this is true, shouldn't feminists be protecting the rights of *all* women to decide what being a woman means to them?

While I was interviewing Phyllis Rippeyoung about her study on the economic cost of breastfeeding,[37] we got fortuitously sidetracked on a discussion about feminism. "For a long time the whole promotion of breastfeeding was this sort of grassroots feminist rejection of Nestlé, and rejection of the commoditization of women's bodies, which as a feminist I can get on board with," the self-described "feminist since third grade" said. "But at the same time it became this enormous pressure . . . and it's like we can relinquish state responsibility for child welfare if we just instead start saying okay, well, women should breastfeed; now it's women's fault that children are growing up with lower IQs. Or say the obesity epidemic . . . any of these things . . . that it's all women's fault. Like child welfare is all on women as opposed to saying we as a society are going to collectively try to address these things, because it impacts everybody's lives."

Maureen Rand Oakley is a political science professor at Mount St. Mary's College who has studied the role of feminism in breastfeeding policy work. She explains that, like pregnancy, breastfeeding is something only women do; this poses a dilemma rooted in what is called the "equality of sameness" concept.

> Under the constitution, the equal protection clause is basically this idea that you are treating people equally under the law. Obviously

> men and women are not exactly the same, but it makes sense in our culture to look at it this way. So then it presents this dilemma—when there are situations where there *are* differences, how do you handle it? As soon as you allow that yes, women are different so maybe policies should be different.... That is what was used against women for so long. They were kept out of jury duty, they were out of all kinds of areas of life, and the justification was always, well, they are first and foremost mothers.[38]

Oakley is in her early forties, and she wonders if part of the disconnect in today's feminist discourse is rooted in generational differences. She says she sometimes worries that her students "take for granted a lot of the things that feminists before them fought for. And so they may not be as worried that by recognizing these differences, that yes, only women breastfeed, and allowing protections and supports for that, that it's going to be used against women ... because they haven't really experienced that sort of thing in their lives."

Oakley nursed her daughter, and also tells me that her mother breastfed in a time when it was far more acceptable to formula feed. She points out the irony of these generational differences. "My mother was not in the workplace. She did not own a second car. Women were home more. This was when they were being urged not to breastfeed. And then just at the time when women are working more, they are out of the home, and they are more likely to have two cars in their household and be able to go out and about and get out of the house, that is when the rise in urging them to breastfeed happens." (Incidentally, Rippeyoung had a similar theory: "It doesn't seem to me to be coincidental that as women in the 1980s—well, you know, you have images of women in power suits and *Working Girl* and all that stuff—that then you sort of have this push back, this backlash of 'go home again.' It's no longer about 'be good to your husband,' but now it's about 'be good to your child.' ")

My generation of parents has worked toward a more egalitarian reality for childrearing. But exclusive breastfeeding leaves women, in the most visceral, embodied sense, as the most appropriate caretaker for infants. So while radical feminists wax poetic about maternal power and releasing ourselves from the old, male-dominated, medicalized version of child nutrition, exclusive breastfeeding also makes truly equal parenting an impossibility. There are certainly other ways fathers can contribute, but if we are going to stress the bonding benefits of infant feeding, we are simultaneously making early nurturing and attachment women's work alone.

Rippeyoung recently began studying the effect of breastfeeding on co-parenting. She came to this research by way of the question: does breastfeeding make it so that the woman becomes the primary parent, and the dad is relegated to "helper" status? "There are all these feminists who say no, it doesn't have to be that way, and then other feminists saying well, that's how it happens." With her colleague Mary Noonan, she carried out research on the fathers of breastfed versus formula-fed kids, and found that "on everything, the dads whose kids are being breastfed relax. When you look at it, it sort of makes sense. It's things like feeding the kid, obviously, but also things like bathing a kid, how often you take the kid to the doctor, how often you get up in the middle of the night, how often you change your baby's diaper . . . and you'd think those are things all dads should do, but when you breastfeed it's like, well, you change the diaper and then you breastfeed. Or if you take them to the doctor to get shots, breastfeeding is going to comfort the baby. So you can kind of understand where those patterns happen." She stresses that by the time the kids are two, a lot of these patterns disperse, although in cases where the mother breastfeeds longer, "there are a few things, like the soothing activities . . . the moms do become more of the soother. The dad soothes less if their partner breastfed a long time."[39]

When my friend Megan was four months into exclusive breastfeeding, she found herself growing aggravated by the oversimplification of parenting roles within the feminist community. "I keep hearing these things about how if you're in a truly feminist, truly 'modern' marriage, then breastfeeding shouldn't lead to an unfair division of labor," she explained to me, sitting on my bed while she nursed her deliciously chubby son. "And I have to say, it's a load of crap." Megan's husband made a meager salary working full time as a barista, but they depended on his benefits; she was an independent contractor with no benefits, but they relied heavily on her income to make ends meet. Neither of them could afford to quit their jobs. Not only was she working obscene hours, but she was getting up every few hours at night to nurse, and since her job wasn't conducive to pumping (she tutored teenagers—"try explaining that as a reason for why you need to take fifteen minutes out of an hour-long session," she laughed), she was relegated to frantic pumping while driving to the next student's house in order to keep up her supply and meet her child's needs. The reality was that only *she* could provide breastmilk for her child. Her other reality was that she needed to work in a specific way to keep her family afloat. Formula wasn't an option, either, considering how expensive it was. There was no easy answer, but as Megan pointed out, it was unfair and obtuse to imply that one could both breastfeed exclusively for a year and still have total equality—at least in terms of division of labor—in a marriage.

It's also important to consider a father's unique role in decisions regarding breastfeeding, as it is one that toes a squiggly line between paternal *rights* and paternal*ism.* Although the reality of the situation is that breastfeeding requires little sacrifice on a father's part and tremendous sacrifice and work on the mother's, this is no one's fault but Mother Nature's. Fathers have an equal stake in the well-being of a child who is 50 percent their creation; if men are hit over the head with the message that formula feeding will have deleterious effects on their offspring, they have every reason to encourage their wives to nurse.

I asked the readers of my blog how much say men should have in infant-feeding decisions.[40] No one seemed 100 percent sure what a father's role should be; one reader worried that "if a man truly believes there is no substitute for breastmilk, and that he's only trying to ensure that his child gets the best, then he might encourage his wife to breastfeed even if it's against her wishes or bad for her health. This is where the 'breast is best' campaign that misleads people into thinking that formula fed babies will be stupid, fat and poisoned really [does] people a disservice." Most felt that ultimately, it needed to be the mother's decision; it was her body. But one woman argued that the best support she got from her husband was when he stepped in and made a decision for her. "When [the struggle to breastfeed] got really bad . . . my husband made the decision for me. He took my son from me and gave him a bottle and when I finally came out of the bedroom the next morning my husband said we weren't breastfeeding anymore," she wrote. "Some may say that what my husband did was wrong, or unsupportive, or even misogynistic . . . but it wasn't. My husband knows *me.* The only way he could have made me stop before I hurt myself or before our child got sick was to make me stop . . . So my husband did an extremely hard thing and he took the stand."[41] Other men feel that the best way to support breastfeeding is to push on through, like you would with any goal. On his blog "How to be a Badass Dad," writer Sol Smith recounts his wife's challenging start to breastfeeding, and urges that the father has a responsibility to "be the stable one": "I wasn't allowed to breakdown in tears or give up. . . . All it would have taken to make the whole project come crashing down would be a small chink in my armor. One moment of hesitation, and I could negatively affect my wife's post-partum, tired, and fed-up will to do the best thing for our baby."[42]

On the other hand, some men do intentionally sabotage their wives' breastfeeding goals. A 1998 study conducted at Ohio State University examined men's negative attitudes toward breastfeeding, and found that "the most common reasons that men gave for not supporting breast-feeding included their fear of separation from the mother, envy of the special bonding between the mother and child and general feelings of inadequacy because only the mother can breast-feed the child."[43] (To counter this, the study's lead author, Rick Petosa, suggested that providers stress the positive aspects of breastfeeding, like "the fact that breast-feeding is not only good for babies, but helps mothers lose weight postpartum"; he seems to be implying that having a slender wife is a fair trade for bonding time with your child.)

Oprah-endorsed Rabbi Shmuley provoked intense rage when he published a piece titled, "Moms, Don't Forget to Feed Your Marriages" on the website Beliefnet.com.[44] "In the end, there are two effects of breast-feeding that we often refuse to acknowledge," Shmuley muses. "One is the de-eroticization of a woman's body, as her husband witnesses one of the most attractive parts of her body serving a utilitarian rather than romantic purpose. This is not to say that breast-feeding isn't sexy. Indeed, the maternal dimension is a central part of womanliness. But public breast-feeding is profoundly de-eroticizing, and I believe that wives should cover up, even when they nurse their babies in their husband's presence." Reading something like that from a well-known relationship "guru" makes a clear case for why those who care about the way women are perceived in our world need to concern themselves with breastfeeding. Breasts are not the sexual real estate of men. But they are also not the property of the state; framing the need to increase breastfeeding rates as a way to improve our nation's health leads to an equally stifling view of women's bodies.

My husband once went on an hour-long diatribe about the stupidity of a bumper sticker we saw that said "Against Child Trafficking." "Is anyone *for* child trafficking?" he shouted at the driver, although our windows were tightly closed. Similarly, I sincerely doubt that most feminists would argue *against* breastfeeding rights or advocacy. But I wonder why more aren't disturbed by how that advocacy is typically carried out. When the message is that *not* breastfeeding is somehow giving in to the man, or makes you less of an actualized, autonomous, or natural mother, doesn't that limit women's choices? For the past several years, although the speakers of the University of North Carolina School of Public Health's annual Symposium on Breastfeeding and Feminism have encompassed a wide range of disciplines and backgrounds, there hasn't been much variety in their philosophies toward breastfeeding promotion. Reading through the available transcripts of past conference proceedings,[45] you notice that there's an eerie sameness to the rhetoric used by every speaker. For example, the focus of the 2007 conference[46] was the DHHS Breastfeeding Campaign brouhaha.

Multiple speakers alluded to the ads being pulled, as if it were a huge disservice to womankind, as if the ads had been pulled solely because of formula industry intervention. I could not find one voice arguing an alternative opinion, bringing up the classist, racist, and misogynist implications of this campaign, or noting that even NOW had broken its underlying code of silence on breastfeeding issues to speak out against the ads. In these proceedings, the only feminist perspective is one that unilaterally supports breastfeeding advocacy and does not believe that "choice" is a valid concept within this debate. There were some intelligent discussions of how the sexualization of breasts (and females, in general) in our society puts nursing women in an uncomfortable position (we're told by medical authorities to breastfeed exclusively, and then made to feel exhibitionist for doing it in public); many speakers focused on the complexities of combining motherhood and work, and others stressed the fracturing of family and "tribal" structures that are beneficial for breastfeeding. The symposium gathered some of the finest and most respected minds of modern feminism—but they all appeared to be of one cohesive mind about an issue that deserves some devil's advocacy.

In its description of the WHO Code, UNICEF applauds Iran for its "innovative" approach to breastfeeding promotion;[47] this innovation entailed making formula a government-controlled substance. With the checkered history of women's rights in Iran, this is troubling on a number of levels. Feminist breastfeeding advocates have chosen to politely ignore dichotomous endorsements such as this, seeming to favor the goal of making the world formula-free over that of securing the bodily autonomy of females across the globe, and ensuring that we have a safe and reliable alternative for infant feeding. When viewed as an example of a profit-driven, male-dominated corporation undermining the natural abilities of women to safely feed their babies, the Nestlé scandal seems like an obvious feminist cause; yet, Shirley Gorenstein points out that the ensuing boycott of the Nestlé corporation "did not demand that the company provide . . . a canned or boxed formula which would enable women and men to use the bottle safely"; instead, the boycott

> assumed that restoring breastfeeding as the exclusive way of feeding babies was the right goal. In this situation, the groups from non-traditional societies (where the baby bottle made breastfeeding optional) were reinforcing traditional society's historical gender system (where breastfeeding was done exclusively) while women from traditional societies were moving towards changing or subverting their current gender system. . . . How do we answer the question, is the baby bottle and formula a feminist or anti-feminist technology? We can't answer that question without working through not only the complexity of the context of the situation in which the technology is set, but also the complexity of the situation of the activists.[48]

There are some disturbing parallels to the abortion debate here. One is an argument over reproductive rights while the other concerns child-rearing, but in both cases, the discourse circulates around a woman's right to exert control over her own body. Some feminists have dealt with this conflict by defining *choice*, in this context, as the "rhetoric of choice," simply a clever construct of the formula industry. There can be no real choosing when we are unable to choose freely; the constructs that make breastfeeding so difficult, especially for those in lower socioeconomic groups, make "choice" an irrelevant concept. Marketing formula to vulnerable women plants mistrust of their own bodies, and the practices of non-Baby-Friendly hospitals destroy breastfeeding efforts. By this reasoning, taking away the temptation of formula would allow women to make an unencumbered choice. This may be true in some cases, but it does not negate the fact that making formula a choice we need to fight for and justify does make it a less viable choice, and the harder a choice is to make, the more unlikely it is a choice at all for women in already challenging situations.

Also, the theory that we are unable to choose freely, while sympathetic, implies that we've made the wrong choice. *That there is a wrong choice to make.* (No wonder, then, that women feel the need to defend that choice by giving evidence of how hard they tried not to have to make it—which just perpetuates the belief that if barriers weren't in place, formula would be rendered unnecessary.)

Jessica Valenti, author of *Full Frontal Feminism: A Young Woman's Guide to Why Feminism Matters* and touted as the "poster girl for third-wave feminism" by Salon.com, started a fresh conversation about these issues when she wrote about her frustration with feminist breastfeeding advocacy (and its support of Baby-Friendly initiatives) on her personal blog in the fall of 2011. She critiqued the "condescending attitude that women who formula feed are somehow stupid or have been duped, the assumption that anyone who formula feeds or supports women who do so isn't educated on the issue, and, of course, the shaming inherent in suggesting that formula hurts women (and babies)." Valenti also railed against the "hypocrisy of judging women who choose to formula feed and the way they are made to justify their choice. . . . [W]hat if [a woman] simply didn't want to breastfeed? Isn't that her right, and shouldn't she be equally supported for that decision in the same way a breastfeeding mom is?"[49]

The response was deafening. Valenti's words provoked numerous heated discussions within the Wild West of social media. She was chastised by fellow feminist bloggers—"[Valenti's] statement about [formula] being 'just as healthy' as breastmilk is patently false, and is disputed by every piece of lactation science published by every health organization in the world. This purposeful misrepresentation of facts and truth is incredibly insulting to women. If an educated, privileged white woman still believes that any processed artificial food is exactly as healthy as any living, whole food, then how are people without access to information expected to know the difference? . . . We should NOT be lying to women in order to make them feel good about their choices," one popular blogger wrote in response to Valenti's assertion that formula was a "healthy" choice.[50] Another resented that Valenti invoked the "choice" rhetoric in the first place: "F**k choice. I want liberation. I want my breasts not to be sexualised commodities to be sold back to me, but rather a part of my body which offer pleasure, function, decorativeness, health-giving properties. . . . I want motherhood to be a valuable and valued contribution in the context of my family, community and society. I want breastmilk to be recognised for its health, bonding, economic and empowering properties. THEN you can ask me to choose."[51]

It's no wonder that feminists (and politicians attempting to secure the female vote) have stuck to the issue of workplace pumping rights, if the issue of breastfeeding is destined to be so divisive. It's a safe way to appear "supportive" of breastfeeding without getting caught in the minefield of another ultimately futile debate over the meaning of choice. If we were really interested in protecting all women, we'd look for a way to protect *both* breastfeeding and formula feeding, not as contradictory choices but as complementary ones. If we were really looking at this from a feminist perspective, we would question why we allow the powers that be to focus so much on infant feeding as a panacea for all the world's ills—because by doing so, we are essentially putting all the responsibility on women's shoulders—or breasts, as it were.

Feminist scholar Joan Williams writes, "Feminists need to do what we are always urging others do. We need to recognize that gender is nothing more or less than a social toolkit and that women use these tools in a variety of ways. Women do not all agree just because they are women. To assume so is to take as a premise the error feminists have united to defeat: that biology determines destiny."[52] Until women stop trying to force their own desires on one another, we're going nowhere fast. Acknowledging that, for some, formula feeding may be an instrument of freedom should not negate the fact that the choice to breastfeed isn't always made freely. These are two separate scenarios, which necessitate two separate, but equal, battles—and neither battle should be fought between women.

FIVE

Damn Lies and Statistics

Throughout all the arguing back and forth about the benefits of breastfeeding, we as a society are ignoring the real elephant in the room. Breastfeeding, except in specific circumstances, *is* a better choice. The real question is *how much better?* We should be questioning if it's better enough to justify the pressure we put on women to do it, even if they don't want to or can't; if it's better enough to excuse poor science and a stupefying dismissal of relative risk.

According to the AAP's official statement on breastfeeding, the act of nursing an infant can reduce the risk of nearly every childhood illness. "Research in the United States, Canada, Europe, and other developed countries, among predominantly middle-class populations, provides strong evidence that human milk feeding decreases the incidence and/or severity of diarrhea, lower respiratory infection, otitis media, bacteremia, bacterial meningitis, botulism, urinary tract infection, and necrotizing enterocolitis. There are a number of studies that show a possible protective effect of human milk feeding against sudden infant death syndrome, insulin-dependent diabetes mellitus, Crohn's disease, ulcerative colitis, lymphoma, allergic diseases, and other chronic digestive diseases,"[1] states the AAP's official literature on infant feeding. It's a great sales pitch: no parent wants to see his or her child in pain. If breastfeeding practically guarantees a healthy child, what loving parent would opt for formula?

We certainly loved our son and believed in the benefits of breastfeeding, but in our case breastfeeding had done nothing but make my child—and me—suffer. We would solve one problem and get smacked on the head with another. After I switched to exclusive pumping, Leo gained weight but you could hardly say he was "thriving"—his skin was god-awful—rashy, pale, and scaly—and he was bloated and uncomfortable. He still cried constantly, barely slept, and every one of his diapers was a horror movie unto itself, forebodingly laced with blood and mucous. The doctors suspected food intolerance; I cut out dairy, soy, green leafy vegetables, nuts; my diet was limited mostly to (milk-free) bread and water, but his symptoms persisted. I struggled to fight off a creeping doubt, lined with a hefty dose of resentment. I felt lied to. I felt misled.

Our pediatrician proposed an experiment. We'd give him one day on hypoallergenic formula only. I'd pump as usual, so there'd be plenty of milk for him if this didn't work, and my supply wouldn't be affected. It seemed harmless, so we agreed to give it a try.

The next day, we stood in front of our fridge, staring at the bottles of breastmilk lined up so proudly next to our organic peanut butter and Steve's leftover Chinese food (which I couldn't eat, obviously—it contained soy). "Should we throw it out?" my husband asked. I shook my head, unable to destroy the fruits of my considerable labor. But we both knew the truth. Within a mere twenty-four hours on hypoallergenic formula, our son's skin had cleared, his stomach was no longer distended, and he had barely cried all day. Despite the full stock of breastmilk in the fridge, we'd become a formula-feeding family.

I was able to frame our formula feeding as the result of unavoidable circumstances, but I couldn't deny that the facts were the facts. We'd just had to perform our own risk-benefit analysis: we weighed how miserable breastfeeding was making our child and our family against the risks posed by formula feeding. It was a close call, but formula won—probably more out of sheer desperation than anything else. The prospect of a future filled with more ear infections or the loss of a few IQ points seemed tolerable when balanced against the constant misery (for all three Barstons) making up our present.

The problem with making decisions in the midst of your own personal hell, though, is that once things have settled down, it's far too easy to start Monday-morning quarterbacking. I became obsessed with researching formula feeding online and torturing myself with all the "facts" about the risks involved and all the advantages I was now depriving Leo of, due to my inability (or, according to the more guilt-promoting texts, my unwillingness) to feed him the way nature intended. Some of the cited risks of formula feeding concerned me more than others—for example, the ear infections and gastrointestinal problems were less troubling. The former was something I'd suffered from as a child, and lived to tell the tale; the latter was kind of irrelevant in our case, having a baby whose stomach problems were *resolved* due to formula feeding. But to hear I was giving my son a higher risk of childhood cancers, diabetes, and meningitis? Head, meet oven.

I think I was missing the point, and everyone else seems to be as well. These decisions are never made in a vacuum; some things may be better for the majority, but not for the individual. "How do we put the breast-milk versus formula question into the context of other health choices we make?" asks Rebecca Goldin and her colleagues at the Statistical Assessment Service (STATS), a nonprofit, nonpartisan group aiming to "correct scientific misinformation in the media and in public policy resulting from bad science, politics, or a simple lack of information or knowledge."[2] "We make decisions all the time that incur risks but also have benefits for the individual. We get into cars, risking death and injury; we send our kids to school, risking infections; and we eat foods like hamburgers, risking an assortment of problems, from obesity to E. coli. . . . Our lives are filled with risks, small and large. Not nursing is a small risk, the real question is what it costs (or benefits) you."[3]

Since writing this article back in 2006, Goldin has been accused of the anti-breastfeeding trifecta: she supposedly is in the pockets of the formula industry, hates breastfeeding, and has no idea what she's talking about. Back in reality, where life is not one big conspiracy theory, Goldin has an undergraduate degree from Harvard and a PhD from MIT; along with her work with STATS, she is an associate professor of mathematical science at George Mason University and, at the time we spoke, served on the Science Policy Committee of the American Mathematical Society. She may not be a lactation consultant, but she certainly has the cred to talk about numbers, statistics, and relative risk. As for being sponsored by Big Formula, she has no personal connection to the industry although they have approached her several times, and she has also insisted that STATS remain free of industry funding. And I think you'd be hard pressed to find an anti-breastfeeding, formula zealot who nursed all four of her children. Her point is not that breastfeeding isn't worthwhile, but that we need to acknowledge the real-world meaning of the often daunting statistics unearthed by breastfeeding research.

Goldin has suggested that the media's flawed interpretation of public health–related statistics is due to a general misunderstanding of a number of key factors, including the difference between causation and correlation; the meaning of "statistically significant"; the "prevalence" of a problem; confounding factors; relative versus absolute risk; and the importance of scientific consensus.[4] A quick-and-dirty rundown of these terms should probably be required reading for any new parent; imagine if, rather than *What to Expect When You're Expecting,* an *Intro to Statistics* textbook graced the nightstand of every pregnant woman. We'd all be a lot less neurotic. At the very least, to understand parenting science enough to avoid panic attacks, we need to comprehend *causation versus correlation, relative risk,* and *confounding factors* better than the average journalist does.

The concept of "causation vs. correlation" means that even if two things are related, it doesn't mean one caused the other. For instance, when I flew out to Virginia to meet Goldin, I observed that a lot of people who work for the Transportation Security Administration (TSA) seem angry. One might assume that working for the TSA turns you into an angry person. This isn't necessarily the case. Maybe angry people are attracted to jobs at the TSA, or maybe the person in charge of hiring TSA staff has a sick sense of humor. These are *confounding factors,* variables that are related to the variable being studied, which can either hide a true effect or imply a false one.

According to Goldin, confounding factors are at the crux of most arguments against the validity of breastfeeding science. It's not the most politically correct concept, but, as she explained to me over lunch, "Someone who is so excited to have a kid and obviously has done all the reading will most likely breastfeed, because everything in society right now tells you that it makes you a good mom," whereas somebody who maybe wasn't all that dedicated to parenthood might not go to the trouble; these tendencies carry through and affect all aspects of parenting. It stands to reason that the same mom who breastfeeds exclusively for six months will also attend all her well-baby visits, will either be able to stay home with her child for that half-year or afford in-home childcare, and will be wealthier and more educated. Even in homogenous groups that don't fit this profile, there are marked differences between those who breastfeed and those who don't. During a Vatican conference on breastfeeding, one researcher admitted that even with the best intentions, it is difficult to control for these confounding factors. He cited evidence from a study looking at low-income populations in Houston, one that his group had elected not to publish "because [they] weren't confident that we could deal with some of the issues that were raised." As he told a group of his well-respected peers: "We controlled for socio-economic status in that we recruited only women who were delivering at our public assistance hospital. But when we looked at our two groups, we found that despite our efforts to control for socioeconomic status, the women who elected to breastfeed were taller and had infants with higher birth weights than the women who elected to bottle-feed. This suggests there is some inherent difference, even in a group of homogeneous socioeconomic status, between women who choose to bottle-feed and those who choose to breastfeed."[5]

Since controlled experiments are ethically impossible, the next best things are sibling studies, which look at children in the same family, thus controlling for a myriad of lifestyle and genetic factors right off the bat. Siobhan Reilly and Eirik Evenhouse, married economists who compared breastfed children to their formula-fed brothers and sisters,[6] designed their study to "look at . . . how much of the difference in the outcomes of the two siblings is accounted for by differences in their breastfeeding history." Reilly explains, "You're shedding all the things that differentiate them from kids in other families—you're essentially controlling for all the things they have in common. They may have grown up in the same neighborhood, they had the same parents, their mother had the same educational level, their parents had the same IQ." This cancels out a lot of the background noise that complicates observational breastfeeding studies, by naturally controlling for many confounding factors.

> Now what you don't control for . . . are any differences between the siblings not captured in the data: if one was premature and that explains why she wasn't breastfed and the other one was. . . . But also differences in the family that occurred over the times between the two kids being born—maybe the mother was working a fulltime job when one child was born and she was staying at home with the children and more able to interact with them when the other was born. . . . So those are some of the problems with sibling studies, but the big advantage is you can knock out the effects of a whole lot of variables that you can't observe because you're just looking at the difference between two siblings who share all those conditions.[7]

Reilly, a strong proponent of breastfeeding (and a former breastfeeding mother herself) tells me that, although they "were pretty sure by doing the study, some effects would be clearly supported and others would be clearly dismissed," the couple was "a little surprised to see that almost none of [the effects of breastfeeding] came out large enough that we could say that they survived the differencing methodology." Since sibling studies are as close to randomized, controlled experiments as infant-feeding studies will ever get, these results are startling. Still, Reilly says, "this doesn't mean that those effects aren't real. But they couldn't be clearly identified in our data."[8]

Aside from confounding factors and correlation not meaning causation, the concept of relative risk often confuses those trying to decipher the cost-benefit scenario of breastfeeding. Going back to my travel analogy, on my flight to Virginia we experienced some turbulence. I'm a nervous flier, but I could have soothed myself by remembering that the risk of dying in a plane crash is far lower than the risk of dying in a car accident, and I'd never think twice about getting into a car. As a general rule, we humans don't have a strong grasp on the concept of relative risk. People are more freaked out by turbulence than traffic.

Once I was (safely) on the ground in Virginia, Goldin and I discussed how individual risk/benefit assessments are necessary and valid when making infant-feeding decisions. "One of the things I think is really important is that even if you *are* at risk for a few more ear infections and stomach aches or things like that, if you use formula . . . that's a perfectly reasonable chance for anybody to take, because they'd rather have to deal with that than deal with not sleeping," Goldin mused. "And I think that's a level of decision—'I'm going to choose between sleeping or my kid getting a cold.' The reality is that any number of things involve putting our children at risk. . . . You put your child in the cart in the supermarket and there's a risk that he could pinch a finger."

Toward the end of our conversation, Goldin and I got a bit more personal, discussing our own breastfeeding experiences. After hearing what we had gone through with Leo, she shook her head. "That's where I think the danger is. . . . They're not listening to individual cases. These are children, not statistics. And I think we have a hard time sometimes understanding that. Your son has his own medical story. If you could do a study of all the children who had that exact same medical history, then there would be relevance. The point is that you're outside of the norm, for whatever reason. . . . And I think that's really, really important."[9]

Infant-feeding decisions can't be based solely on what studies say because health is an individual thing. Artificial sweeteners are a godsend for diabetics and those with dental issues. They've also been shown to cause cancer, migraines, and other maladies in lab rats. Good for some; not so good for others. Formula is downright dangerous in areas with a lack of clean water or if prepared improperly; breastfeeding can be dangerous if the mother is on a few select medications or recreational drugs, or if she can't make enough milk. Studies can tell us what may be beneficial for the norm, but a lot depends on what your personal norm may be.

• • •

No one quite knows who said it first,[10] but whoever came up with the saying "lies, damn lies, and statistics" was one smart cookie. Research is a complex beast; it's actually not all about the numbers because it's being conducted by human beings, and whenever there are humans involved, there's human emotion.

The more experts I spoke to about breastfeeding, the more I understood just how much your own personal experiences could color your interpretation of data. The author of one respected, scholarly book on human lactation told me she couldn't relate to the women who said breastfeeding was such hard work. Her sons had been "snackers"; they'd nursed for only a few minutes at a time, so it was no huge time investment. "I guess some babies take longer to breastfeed but still, it's not your whole day. They sleep a lot. It's a lot easier than adult children," she said archly. This was similar to arguments I'd had with friends as our children entered the toddler years; some of the moms in our group mourned the loss of babyhood as their kids grew more mobile, more verbal, and consequently more defiant. I couldn't fathom this perspective because Leo's worst terrible two tantrum was nothing compared to the hell we lived through during his infancy. It's all a matter of perspective.

The media might be guilty of misrepresenting data; the medical community could be chastised for being overly cautious. But I'd propose that the chief problem of the breastfeeding debate, inherent in this misguided presentation of "facts," is that even those who do have the education and professional background to "know better" can easily get misled by their own fears, insecurities, and emotions. We laypeople take it on faith that scientific research is impartial, but this is far from the truth—especially when we're talking about public health concerns. Mary Renfew, for example, is the author of an impressive number of lauded breastfeeding studies. A professor of maternal and infant nutrition at the University of York, she's crystal clear about her personal feelings regarding breastfeeding. "[There] has been a huge force for good trying hard to counter . . . societal forces so that women can do what women are, in part, born to do. They are born to do many other things too, but one of them is breastfeed the baby," she told a group of like-minded individuals during a conference on infant feeding.[11] If someone has an empirical belief that women are in fact born to breastfeed—that it is integral to their identity or validity as women—how can that not color her judgment?

The Encyclopedia of Public Health warns:

> Many public health scientists are willing to become advocates, taking a public position in favor of actions that will reduce or eliminate risks to health that their scientific studies have disclosed. But many other public health scientists are not prepared to become advocates, arguing that by doing so they would compromise their scientific objectivity. They assert that if they become public health advocates they cease to be impartial and thereby compromise future scientific studies that they may undertake . . . that a conflict of interests will arise if they become advocates for a particular cause in public health practice. Scientific objectivity is often equated with impartiality, which, by definition, is incompatible with advocacy, which necessarily adopts a position in favor of or against a particular cause.[12]

Scientists are human, of course; it's naïve to think that bias doesn't enter the research field. That's the purpose of metastudies or reviews, which examine a wide variety of studies in the hope of seeing a trend. Breastfeeding research finds its strength in metastudies, which do tend to show a consistent protective effect against several ailments like ear infections and gastrointestinal infections. Other breastfeeding benefits do not show up as consistent "truth" throughout the research landscape—and yet, these are mentioned consistently as if they have been proven beyond any doubt.

Nearly every paper I read discussing the tendency to overstate breastfeeding benefits cited the work of Jules Law, whose quintessential article "The Politics of Breastfeeding" critiques the "circular" nature of breastfeeding science. "All too often, scientific research into the consequences and effects of infant feeding choices concludes by acknowledging the inconclusiveness of its own results but then recommends breastfeeding on the grounds that its virtues are already well established in any case," he writes.[13]

Law's field of expertise is not sociology, epidemiology, medicine, or even feminism—it's comparative literature. He became interested in the breastfeeding discourse while working on a book about how bodily fluids are portrayed historically through literature.

> I started doing research on nineteenth-century attitudes towards wet nursing. . . . So I found the one academic book on the history of breastfeeding[14] and I got detoured a little, because I was struck by a moment in that book where the author claims that seventeenth-century women who put their kids out to wet nurse did so for the sake of convenience, in the same "often unthinking" way—this book is written back in the 1980s—that women today bottle feed. I thought she was going to cite research or archival evidence that would allow her to characterize women's attitudes towards breastfeeding and wet nursing in that way, but it turns out that she was just making assumptions about why seventeenth-century women put children out to a wet nurse, just as she was assuming, wrongly, that she knew why women bottle-fed [in her day]. But now of course, her work gets cited by people who want to argue that these are the attitudes that women had in the seventeenth century, and their agenda in turn is to show that if women today have the same attitudes as women in the seventeenth century, then those attitudes must be trans-historical and natural. . . . I started getting interested in the breastfeeding discourse. . . . I got obsessed with how much this kind of circular logic pervaded all the available literature, scholarly and nonscholarly.[15]

In his article, Law illustrates the danger of this "circular logic," using the example of what was, at the time, "the most sensational current figure circulating among breastfeeding advocates": a statement that eight thousand infant deaths per year in the United States were attributable to formula feeding.

> This figure is extraordinary and completely lacking in scientific foundation or documentation. All references to it extrapolate from a single 1989 "study" conducted by the National Institute of Environmental Health Sciences (NIEHS). But the actual source is simply a one-paragraph abstract of a study of carcinogens in breast milk (Rogan 1989). Neither the abstract nor the study itself purports to analyze formula feeding. Nonetheless, in order to contextualize the relative risk of carcinogens in breast milk, the abstract postulates an alternative risk of 4-in-1,000 deaths attributable to formula feeding. The figure is never mentioned again—let alone explained or corroborated. . . . Thus breastfeeding advocates have cited a misreported figure, which, moreover, was derived from a study that did not collect or examine any data on actual infant-feeding practices. Yet this figure now circulates in breastfeeding-advocacy literature as the scientifically established "result" of a "study" by NIEHS.[16]

"It's one thing for laypeople to think of science as a religion or to have a kind of mystified view of it," Law tells me when I ask him how his foray into breastfeeding research affected his views of science. "But for scientists, rather than saying, 'our data actually don't really prove much,' to say, 'Well, you know the data only points *slightly* in a certain direction, but it's in the direction we would have expected it to point anyways, so this probably does confirm our reigning assumptions.' . . . That's very disturbing. . . . I was kind of shocked at that."

Joan Wolf, author of *Is Breast Best? Taking on the Breastfeeding Experts and the New High Stakes of Motherhood*[17] (which earned her comparisons to advocates of cold fusion and Holocaust deniers, simply because she offered a different perspective on the research), has argued that the "experts" we rely on to accurately assess breastfeeding research have stopped asking the question

> of whether or not there's proof for [the claims made about breastfeeding]. We've become so persuaded. How it is that doctors and scientists have essentially become convinced that breast is best? Part of it is information overload and your reliance on other people for information . . . you know, you can't go out and do the research yourself. And, when everybody keeps saying that breast is best you start saying it too. You're relying on other people to evaluate information for you, and they're also relying on other people and so . . . it ends up being that everybody believes one thing and there's only one person who's actually looked at it.[18]

Wolf acknowledges that "breastfed babies tend to be healthier; they tend to be slightly smarter," but she doesn't think that science has conclusively shown us that it's the breastmilk itself that is conferring these benefits. "When you see an association (between breastfeeding and better outcomes) five hundred times, you begin to think there's something to it. But if you have a flawed study that comes up with this result and you redo that same study five hundred times, you're no closer to the answer than you were in the beginning. If you repeat the error five hundred times you still have lousy data."[19]

"Lousy data" can spread like a virus: in the second decade of the new millennium, obesity and breastfeeding have become seductively intertwined, despite a lack of conclusive data that breastfeeding truly has a "protective effect" against fatness. First Lady Michelle Obama made breastfeeding an integral part of her plan to fight childhood obesity, claiming in February 2011 that "because it's important to prevent obesity early, we're also working to promote breastfeeding, especially in the black community—where 40 per cent of our babies never get breastfed at all, even in the first weeks of life. . . . We know that babies that are breastfed are less likely to be obese as children."[20]

Know may be too strong a word, considering the shaky science behind these claims. It's true that several studies have suggested a correlation between children who are breastfed and a lower chance of being overweight, but others have found no significant link. In fact, the research Obama was likely referring to—a 2007 Agency for Healthcare Research and Quality (AHRQ) report,[21] which the surgeon general in her husband's administration had used to form a new "Call to Action on Breastfeeding"[22] in 2011—cautions that although there is "an association between a history of breastfeeding and a reduction in the risk of being overweight or obese in adolescence and adult life . . . one should be cautious in interpreting all these associations because of the possibility of residual confounding." In plain speak, the report states that although a few studies have shown an advantage (and a small one at that—a 4 percent reduction in risk is probably not worth basing a whole campaign on) to breastfeeding in combating obesity, these studies have also been rife with confounding factors and the benefit is not entirely clear.

An earlier metastudy, published in 2001, found conflicting evidence; two studies referenced even seemed to suggest that breastfeeding could be *positively* correlated with later obesity. The authors summarize that "most studies examining the effects of breastfeeding on later obesity have found an insignificant effect. . . . An effect of breastfeeding on later obesity, if any, is probably weaker than genetic and other environmental factors. . . . Although a highly provocative concept, the protective effect of breastfeeding on later obesity remains controversial."[23] And a 2003 cross-sectional study that examined several generations found "no support for a protective effect of breast feeding on obesity."[24] The authors also point out that "secular trends do not suggest a protective effect: in both Britain and the United States the incidence of breast feeding has increased since 1990, but so has obesity. Promoting breast feeding is important, but evidence for an important beneficial effect on obesity is still equivocal."

Even Michael Kramer, the physician/researcher responsible for what is probably considered the best breastfeeding-related study in recent history (the Promotion of Breastfeeding Intervention Trial, or PROBIT, performed in the country of Belarus),[25] admits that the obesity benefit is probably minimal. At a 2008 American Society for Nutrition conference (which was, admittedly, funded by the International Formula Council), he reported that according to his well-regarded research, breastfeeding did not reduce the development of obesity at 6.5 years of age.[26]

Despite the paucity of good-quality, definitive research, the breastfeeding-prevents-obesity myth will not die. Perhaps this is because it goes hand in hand with a complementary claim: that formula feeding *causes* kids to become overweight. (It doesn't matter to the myth's promoters that formula feeding is also associated with lower income,[27] which is strongly correlated with obesity[28]—again, this comes down to correlation versus causation.) Formula has become a scapegoat for our nation's obesity epidemic, and out of a belief in this association has sprung the phenomenon of "obese babies." Infant chubbiness has become a medical problem; what used to be considered cute is now a health threat. The danger in this, of course, is that health-conscious formula-feeding parents can become so fearful of overfeeding that they deprive their babies of essential nutrition. In Bellevue, Washington, a mother was arrested for allegedly starving her daughter because "her husband [had] a weight problem and [she] did not want her girls to be fat." "I was so concerned she was gaining the weight so fast. I didn't care that she was gaining the weight. That is fine. But too fast, it scared the crap out of me," the woman said in an interview in January 2010.[29]

Considering that parents had recently been warned that rapid weight gain in infancy leads to later obesity, based on a study that was published in the April 2009 issue of *Pediatrics*,[30] this wasn't all that surprising. Now, I'm not saying that I withheld food from Leo after the results of this study hit the newsstands, but I did start feeling anxious every time someone commented on his "chub." I had a few friends whose babies were even chunkier than my little Buddha, but they were all breastfeeding. A few times, people who assumed I was nursing made comments like "good job, mama!" in regard to Leo's girth; I'd blush, hoping that they wouldn't notice the bottle sticking out of my diaper bag. If I were breastfeeding, there would be no question that Leo was gaining the way he was supposed to, but since I "controlled" his food intake through his bottles, it was my fault if he was gaining too much, too fast. I would think that with the current fat-phobic climate, this sort of paranoia regarding infant weight gain is pandemic.

ABC's *Good Morning America* (GMA) reported a trend of parents putting babies on "diets," which the show suggested might be in response to this same study.[31] But even in that news report, which condemned the practice of withholding food from infants based on one study, the formula-feeding scare tactics were in full force. "We need to stop the notion that fat, cuddly, cute babies are a good thing," GMA quoted one pediatrician as saying. "The answer, however, is not to put your baby on a diet. Rather, the best start for a baby is breast-feeding. . . . Breast-fed babies tend to gain weight faster early on and then slow down in the next six months. . . . Formula-fed babies tend to continue the rapid weight gain as a result of overfeeding or inappropriate feeding by their parents." Notice that there are no *ifs, ands,* or *buts* used in this passage—it is implied that *all* formula-fed babies will continue the rapid weight gain; that they *all* will be fed inappropriately. Semantics, perhaps. But regardless, it perpetuates the unfounded belief that formula feeding "causes" fatness, and potentially sets bottle-feeding parents up for a major complex—despite the fact that these claims are based on equivocal evidence. Plus, even if it is true that kids who grow faster in infancy have an increased risk for being slightly more overweight than their peers, there may also be some advantages to being "overfed." The same physician quoted for the GMA story explains that "babies who gain weight at the higher percentiles have better neurocognitive outcome, less lung disease, but run the risk of later adverse outcomes such as diabetes and hypertension. . . . Babies who grow at the lower percentiles run the risk of lower neurocognitive outcome and more lung disease, but less risk for adverse outcomes."

Fat, or stupid and wheezy? Pick your poison.

• • •

In some ways, relying purely on observational studies, without any real understanding of the biological mechanisms that confer such amazing benefits on breastfed babies, is not much more "scientific" than anecdotal evidence. Yet saying "my formula kid never gets sick" or "I was formula fed, and I turned out fine" will get you nowhere. You'll be told that your child may have long-term problems that you just aren't aware of yet, or that he or she is a lucky fluke. To be fair, this critique is correct: anecdotal evidence is pretty worthless. On the other hand, certain studies are really just a ton of anecdotes collected into one place and thrown into a computer program meant for statistical assessment. These anecdotes are called "self-reported data" in the research world. Self-reported data isn't *quite* as unreliable as true anecdotal evidence, since researchers can reduce the effect of bias within study parameters; in fact, the use of self-reported data in public health research is extremely common and entirely acceptable. Good examples of what is considered high-quality self-reported data are the Nurses' Health Study II (NHSII) and its predecessor, the original Nurses' Health Study (NHS).[32] These are collections of self-reported data from a group of female nursing professionals of childbearing age, from a variety of states across the country. NHS and NHSII ask women a myriad of health-related questions via questionnaires that are mailed to the participants every few years.

NHS and NHSII have been used for breastfeeding-related studies, like those associating breastfeeding with lowered diabetes[33] and breast cancer risk,[34] both heralded as ways in which breastfeeding benefits mothers. Yet, researchers have worried about the validity of self-reported data. "In epidemiological studies, questionnaires and interviews are often the only feasible means by which information can be obtained," explains the introduction to a study examining the accuracy of recollection in the nurses involved in the NHS. "Self-reported data, like data obtained by sources external to the study participants, can be afflicted by biases and misclassification."[35]

This bias isn't even necessarily the kind of bias we typically worry about. It's not that people's opinions on something like breastfeeding color their responses (although responses can be vividly painted by "social desirability bias," or the tendency to want to give information that we think is socially acceptable);[36] the more innocent phenomena of "selection bias" and "recall bias" can really screw up results. When Walter Willett, an epidemiologist who has worked extensively with NHS and NHSII, was interviewed for the website ScienceWatch, he told a story that illustrates the power of these biases. During a study on the association of past dietary fat intake and breast cancer using the NHS women, Willett and his associates noticed some discrepancies in the data.

> Depending on whether we asked about diet before or after the diagnosis of breast cancer, we obtained a different answer. Had we relied solely on the case-control data, we would have concluded that there's a positive association between fat intake and breast cancer. But in the prospective analysis, there was absolutely no relationship. That shows that this combination of selection bias—in other words, who participates in the controls—plus the recall bias can produce some bias [in results]. What we saw was a modest bias, but we're looking for a modest effect, so it was enough to seriously distort the data.[37]

Another researcher, interviewed for the *New York Times* about a study conducted via self-reported data suggesting an increased risk of birth defects in children conceived through fertility treatments, explained that "when you send questionnaires, the tendency is for the couple who may have had a problem or who think they have a problem to answer that questionnaire. . . . Those who do not respond tend to be parents whose children seem fine, skewing the data."[38]

Studies can avoid some of the pitfalls of recall bias by using external sources of data to back up what subjects are reporting—things like medical records and lab tests—but not all studies do this, and that is why it's important to understand just how researchers reach the conclusion they broadcast. That's difficult when most of us need to rely on the media to accurately report the studies, or pay thirty bucks a pop to download the actual papers from medical journals (assuming you have the ability to understand the medical and epidemiological jargon, as well as the time to read through all the referenced citations . . . which of course, is *entirely* possible in the five minutes you have during nap time that's not filled with scrambling around to wash your dishes and take the dog out).

Still, not all breastfeeding studies are based on self-reported data, and some really do rely on sound science. And it's almost irrelevant to overanalyze the studies or question that in most cases, breast is better than bottle, because it's a fight only the formula companies care about winning. What *is* relevant is making sure women are not pressured, for the "good of humanity," into doing something that should be a personal choice, especially when the risks involved are dramatically misunderstood or misrepresented.

Consider if every parenting decision we made were based on this narrow interpretation of relative risk. Parents might be warned not to have babies via in-vitro fertilization, because babies conceived through IVF have an increased risk of childhood and adult cancers; are "seven times more likely to be born with a set of rare urological birth defects that include the formation of the bladder outside the body,"[39] and triple the risk of autism.[40] Women could be alerted to the dangers of getting pregnant with an older partner's sperm, since studies have shown that kids with older fathers have decreased cognitive ability and an increased risk of autism and birth defects.[41] Working mothers, be warned—your child may do worse in school and have an increased risk of unemployment and psychological stress, according to a recent British study.[42] Even gaining a little too much weight during pregnancy—especially if you were thinner to begin with—can make your kid 48 percent more likely to be obese at the age of seven.[43]

"You know, it's probable that on balance there is a very slight marginal health advantage to breastfeeding, so you'd have to weigh that relative to other things that impinge upon your baby and your family," Jules Law muses. "For a lot of people, that's a heretical, horrendously impersonal, inhumane way of talking about your relationship with your baby. But what's wrong with talking in terms of assessing how much of an advantage it is? What's wrong with saying you might actually choose not to pursue that particular advantage in order to pursue other advantages within the general framework of the health and welfare of your family life, which includes, of course, your baby? But that kind of pragmatic thinking is seen as kind of inhumane."[44] *Inhumane* might seem like a strong term, but when we're being told that our choice to formula feed is costing America thirteen billion dollars and killing 911 of our children every year, mothers are in effect being held responsible for the health and wealth of the nation. Rather than a simple, personal matter of relative risk, it has become about formula-feeding mothers contributing to a public health threat of daunting proportions.

These frightening figures come from a 2009 study titled "The Burden of Suboptimal Breastfeeding in the United States: A Pediatric Cost Analysis," which appeared in *Pediatrics*, the medical journal published by the AAP, giving it instant credibility. It sparked a media frenzy, stating in its abstract (which, according to Wolf, is often all physicians—and presumably pressed-for-time journalists—read of any study)[45] that "if 90% of US families could comply with medical recommendations to breastfeed exclusively for 6 months, the United States would save $13 billion per year and prevent an excess 911 deaths, nearly all of which would be in infants. . . . Current US breastfeeding rates are suboptimal and result in significant excess costs and preventable infant deaths."[46]

Headlines screamed bloody murder—literally. "More breastfeeding could save 900 lives a year!" yelled CBS News.[47] "Lack of breastfeeding costs lives; billions of dollars," warned CNN.[48] Apparently, this study had shown that "if most new moms would breastfeed their babies for the first six months of life, it would save nearly 1,000 lives and billions of dollars each year."[49] If this had truly been the case, the media could certainly justify their dramatic reporting of the study. But the results were not nearly as cut-and-dried as the articles made them out to be.

"This isn't a typical health study," explains psychologist, blogger, former researcher, and "mother against distorted data" Polly Palumbo.[50] "[The authors] don't critically examine whether breastfeeding actually prevents disease. In fact they take it for granted and pull ten health conditions linked to breastfeeding from [the 2007 AHRQ report],[51] a government review based on studies done mainly in the 1980s and 1990s." The authors then estimated the health care costs associated with treating the resulting conditions—everything from doctor visits to medications, and more indirect costs like parental work absences. They then compared this to what they *estimated* would happen if 80 percent to 90 percent of women breastfed exclusively for six months.

Says Palumbo,

> They took a very large leap or two in calculating these costs. First they estimated how many deaths resulted each year (for each condition) due to "suboptimal breastfeeding"—even though the [AHRQ] report concluded there was insufficient data to calculate premature deaths. But the authors never reveal how they actually estimated the number of "premature" deaths. They report how they calculated everything else, but not the deaths. . . . Basically they blamed each death entirely on suboptimal breastfeeding. The corollary, then, is that more breast milk would prevent children from dying. Now, that just isn't accurate. It might prevent some children from getting the disease in question (although that's not

> completely clear either) but it's a stretch to say not breastfeeding was *entirely* responsible for deaths. It's also possible there are factors that make breastfeeding difficult for a child and also contribute to death, like chronic health conditions.[52]

She also cautions that "the authors don't approach the literature on breastfeeding from a neutral standpoint. Even if it's rightly recognized as the preferred choice, the authors' bias is clear from the 'burden of suboptimal breastfeeding' in the title to their conclusion endorsing the 'creation of a national infrastructure to support breastfeeding.' "

Palumbo worries about the impact of this study. "Reading about the 900 baby deaths . . . that can get to a parent. As for the health professional who may be more convinced by medical costs, they now have that 13 billion and those dead babies to use in their arguments for breastfeeding. Yet the estimates are deceiving and dramatic, and will be cited over and over."

Palumbo has good reason to worry. These findings weren't questioned; the media reported the numbers as fact, without stopping to consider how the numbers were calculated, or even what the numbers meant in the grand scheme of things. Rebecca Goldin tried to offer a modicum of common sense when she was interviewed by ABC News, critiquing the "13 billion in savings" aspect for failing to factor in the social and professional costs that a nursing mom—and a society that did what it needed to in order to allow women to nurse exclusively for six months—might accrue. "When you do an economic comparison, it's unfair to only look at one aspect of the cost for any one particular decision. It's not clear that this is a fair savings to the nation," she told ABC, explaining that "studies like the current one present a problem for women who can't afford or otherwise choose not to pay those costs of breastfeeding, because often they are looked upon poorly." She also "asserted that driving could be made to look equally bad, given the medical costs in the form of car accidents" and asked if it would be fair to "look at the medical costs of driving and talk about the morality of driving."[53]

A few days after the ABC News report came out, I noticed Goldin's name popping up on several lactivist blogs, including on the website of one prominent, mainstream breastfeeding advocacy group. This organization wrote a response to the ABC piece, condemning them for spreading misinformation and picking apart the "expert" quotes from Goldin and another female physician (who did, in fact, have links to the formula industry). There was nothing outwardly accusatory toward Goldin in the group's original piece, but in an online discussion one of the organization's founders casually mentioned that "apparently, Dr. Goldin is related to the formula industry too. No wonder moms trust blogs more than the mainstream media."[54]

When I contacted her to ask where she'd gotten this information, she quickly responded, "[Dr. Goldin's quotations] in the ABC News article don't hold water, which is why I wrote this post. Her position is sufficiently outlandish that it draws attention to her and invites critical examination both of her work, and of the institutions with which she is affiliated, by researchers and scientists we respect (the information we received came from a national watchdog organization). But I am less interested in going down the rabbit hole of her affiliations and prefer to stick to the confusing points she made in this story. . . . I hope you will join me in questioning her position on this issue, as it serves neither breastfeeding nor formula-feeding mothers."[55]

Lies, damn lies, and statistics. Amen.

• • •

Ultimately, even if we take the science for what it is, there is still a plethora of unanswered questions and conspicuous gaps in our understanding of infant nutrition. When we spoke, Joan Wolf expressed frustration at the limited scope of breastfeeding research. "Let's get the lactation scientists to try to figure out what would have to happen in the body for the breast milk to be making a difference. If breast milk truly reduces the chance that you will get diabetes, tell me how that happens biologically. Let's work on that instead of doing another five hundred studies on whether or not breastfeeding is associated with diabetes."[56]

To perform a study like this, we'd have to use two sample groups—one that was exclusively pumping and feeding breastmilk in bottles, and another that was predominately feeding from the breast. Depending on these results, we could infer whether the benefit was coming from the milk or some aspect of the breastfeeding experience. If it was the milk that was indeed preventing diabetes, then a separate study could be undertaken to try to decipher which element of breastmilk was doing so. This ingredient could then possibly be created synthetically and added to formula, giving women (and babies) an alternative—not as a way to replace or disparage breastfeeding as a practice, but simply to focus on the end rather than the means; to free women from biological imperatives and give them choices that didn't force them to feel they were putting their own needs before their children's.

What if, rather than asking women to bear the burden of responsibility for our nation's health and intelligence, governments invested money in research for better formulas that can improve health? If what we feed our babies in the first year *really* has that much of an impact on lifelong health, this should be a priority. Because in reality, not all babies are going to be able to be breastfed, as long as we want to live in a world where women have the freedom to decide how to use their bodies; whether to work or stay home; whether to be a primary caregiver or not. In reality, there are going to be children raised by single dads; there are going to be children raised by grandparents; there are going to be children who are adopted by parents who aren't able to induce lactation; there are going to be children whose mothers don't produce enough milk, or who are on drugs not compatible with breastfeeding. Rather than demanding that every mother should be able to—should *want to*—breastfeed, we should be demanding better research, better resources, better options.

We should be demanding *better*.

SIX

Soothing the Savage Breast

I had only one friend who chose to formula feed from the beginning, without ever bringing her child to her breast. Erin's husband had been deployed in Iraq when she gave birth to her first son, and she'd started out thinking that she would attempt to breastfeed, but "being a single working mom with a job that was less than breastfeeding friendly in nature was overwhelming" and Erin started thinking that it would be too much for her to handle. She worried that she would be depriving her son by not giving breastfeeding the old college try.

> Everything came to a head one night as I was cooking with my brother [a chef] . . . and he imparted the only piece of parenting advice he has ever shared with me. He started talking about the recipe he was working on and how when he cooks he prefers to use eggs from a specific local organic farm but that sometimes he just can't get those eggs—delivery problems, the chickens don't lay eggs, whatever. In those circumstances he can't just close the restaurant or refuse to make specific dishes that use eggs; he has to use other eggs. Eggs that are just as good in a lot of ways and most importantly, still do the job that needs to be done in the recipe. And while the

> yolks may not be as yellow or the eggs as fresh in general, the end result is still just as good. . . . I had the realization that parenting is a lot like cooking. There are many ingredients that go into making a meal, just like there are many decisions that we make as parents. And even if you can't necessarily get the one ingredient you think you need to make a meal work, you can find a substitute that will make something just as delicious. . . . [U]sing formula is only one part of what I do as a mother, and not something that will define me or my relationship with my son.

Erin's story didn't end there. Her husband returned from his deployment and she got pregnant again. And this time, with the advantage of a co-parent and not having to work, she was able to breastfeed her second son. "Do I think I made the right decision for my second son? Yes. I believe that just as strongly as I still believe that I made the right decision for my first son when I gave him formula from the very start. Different circumstances, different children, and different decisions that were equally right for me, my child, and our family."

Like Erin, mothers are not "breastfeeders" or "formula feeders," but rather women who choose to feed their babies in the best way possible for their given situation. Defining ourselves by what we feed our child for the first year is as insane as defining ourselves by how that child was conceived, and you don't see too much mainstream rage between those who had children via fertility treatments or adoption and those who "naturally" conceived. So why is this fight so vitriolic?

Those who are attempting to make breastfeeding the norm have a tough row to hoe, especially in a culture where every baby doll comes accessorized with a bottle. Even in 2011, when "there is no debate" about the superiority of breastmilk, women are still being kicked out of malls for nursing, given hell about taking pumping breaks at work, and being banned from posting photos on Facebook of nursing infants. If I had suffered any of these injustices, I'd be royally ticked off, too. Especially when the medical community pushes us so hard to breastfeed, and our cultural climate puts ultimate responsibility on mothers for the future health of the nation . . . and then those same forces turn on us if we nurse too long or too indiscreetly. It's more than unfair; it's despicable.

I've overheard many breastfeeding mothers expressing frustration about the fact that whenever they rail against a bottle-feeding culture, formula companies, or formula-pushing physicians, their formula-feeding peers accuse them of "making moms feel guilty." They have a point. Even online articles in respected publications get their fair share of this phenomenon. Mention the benefits of breastfeeding in an online arena and you're guaranteed at least one or two comments about how someone couldn't breastfeed and her child is just as brilliant and amazing as anyone else's. On one popular parenting blog, a reader angrily complained that "women who are passionate about breastfeeding and promote breastfeeding by talking about the facts are constantly under attack. When are mothers going to stop fighting with each other?" But as she continued, she unknowingly answered her own question. "When are people going to stop making all kinds of false accusations and start thinking about what really matters—the health and welfare of our children and ultimately our population?"[1]

Unfortunately, statements like that are exactly *why* women feel attacked by breastfeeding advocacy. Even if one agrees that breastfeeding will have a significant public health impact, it's hard to justify that logic to a mom who is struggling in that moment. Public health efforts must subjugate the needs of the individual for the good of the whole, but tell that to a mom who feels like throwing her child across the room when she nurses, due to flashbacks of abuse. Or a mom whose baby gets sicker and sicker on breastmilk, no matter what she cuts from her diet. Or a mom whose preemie—a child who would not have survived before the advent of the same medical advances that apparently led to a formula-feeding culture—is unable to latch and loses precious weight.

Emotion fuels both sides of this "debate." Just as defensiveness might color a formula-feeding mom's interpretation of the infant-feeding discourse, some breastfeeding advocates will understandably see formula as the enemy. In 2011, after her publication of a review article on infant-feeding disaster preparedness, breastfeeding activist Karleen Gribble engaged in an enlightening and lively debate on FearlessFormulaFeeder.com. One of the points of contention between Gribble and my readers was that in her article she neglected to point out how much safer ready-to-feed, single-use "nursers"[2] would be in an emergency situation (these would negate the need for sterilization, clean water, bottle washing, etc.). She argued that these were not available in all countries; I suggested that formula companies would most likely be happy to donate the proper supplies, even if they weren't typically available in the country where the disaster occurred—it would be a much-needed boon to their precarious reputations. During the rather heated discussion that ensued, she informed me that donations were not welcome from formula companies and commented that "UNICEF's sponsorship policy places companies that breach the International Code of Marketing of Breastmilk Substitutes as more untouchable than tobacco companies because of the impact of their unethical marketing practices on the well-being of children. They

[UNICEF] purchase what they need at market prices." Gribble was not speaking on UNICEF's behalf; I have no idea whether UNICEF would accept donations from formula manufacturers in a time of dire need, but considering their stance on the WHO Code, Gribble is most likely correct.

What Nestlé and other formula companies have done in third-world countries is unforgivable, but we can't allow the heartless marketing practices of profit-driven corporations to warp our common sense. If a disaster were to happen tomorrow in an area where breastfeeding rates are low, formula would be needed. It is irrelevant that breastfeeding would be a more economical and safer option (because there is no doubt it would be; as long as the mother was adequately hydrated and not in an extreme state of starvation, she could sustain her child for a significant amount of time; formula feeding would require the proper supplies and adequate resources); if a baby is not in proximity to a willing, lactating woman, we better hope that he's in arm's reach of some Good Start. There's a reason why people sign deals with the devil in all of those 1980s movies: when you're in desperate need of something, you don't really have the luxury to care about morality.

If there weren't enough reasons to hate what Nestlé and other formula companies did in the third world, I'll submit one more: their actions have caused a reverse halo effect, making it difficult for some to separate the product from the producer. Formula as a substance did not convince women that their bodies weren't capable of nurturing life; marketing executives, injustices, and bad circumstances did a bang-up job of that all on their own. Formula as a substance does not kill babies; the water used to reconstitute it does—rather than blame the powder sitting in the can, we should be blaming the infrastructure.

Unfortunately, even if we are capable of viewing formula purely as a substance, it will still be seen as a competitor to breastmilk. No wonder, then, that some breastfeeding moms might view it negatively; it's a substance that renders considerable efforts unnecessary and allows society to criticize them for their choices. But part of viewing formula as a *substance* is realizing that formula is an entirely separate entity from formula *feeders,* or the act of formula *feeding.* Women who choose to—or have to—formula feed are not necessarily anti-breastfeeding; in fact, many of them are wholeheartedly in favor of the practice. For most formula-feeding women, formula doesn't hold the same meaning as breastmilk. We see it as food, not the magical elixir breastmilk may or may not be, and not an outright rejection of the beauty and power of breastfeeding. I can't speak for every formula feeder in the world, but personally, hearing that breast is "normal" or "best" doesn't offend me at all. It wasn't "normal" or "best" to need progesterone to carry a pregnancy to term, but *I* needed it, and that progesterone allowed me the gift of my children. Formula may not be perfect, but for those who cannot make breastfeeding work, for any reason, this substance gives us the ability to nourish our kids—and that is something to be grateful for.

There are lactivists who understand this distinction, and their positive approach would be far more effective than the current modus operandi. "I think if breastfeeding advocacy focused on *breastfeeding* rather than comparing it to formula it [would be] best served. You can spread awareness on the benefits of breastfeeding, the ways to overcome any hurdles, without talking about formula," argues Devan McGuinness-Snider, a well-known blogger and breastfeeding advocate.[3] Natural parenting blogger Suchada Eickemeyer agrees, using the metaphor of a

Thanksgiving meal to explain her feelings on the breastmilk/formula divide. "I'm a turkey person myself, and I can't really imagine serving Tofurky for Thanksgiving dinner, but people have all kinds of reasons for doing it," she writes.

> The place for change is with the people who want to serve turkey, but are intimidated by all the methods (roasting, frying, smoking), the endless instructions (trussing, basting, turning), the horror stories of how it can go wrong (frozen in the middle, overcooked and dry), and decide Tofurky might be the easier, and therefore best, option. If we can spread the word that you just have to thaw it out a few days before, and then pop it in the oven for a few hours, it might change some minds. But talking about how crappy Tofurky is when they reluctantly decide to serve it will just ruin their Thanksgiving.[4]

If breastfeeding advocacy continues to fuel itself on negativity and zealotry, rather than listening to astute voices such as these, its proponents will be ruining more than a poultry-sacrificing holiday. As it is, the push to breastfeed in America is creating a strong push *back.* One of my blog readers told me that although when she first switched to formula she "felt absolutely horrible . . . like I was just the worst person in the world . . . like I was going to be judged by everyone any time I pulled out my baby's bottle . . . like I had failed her," that guilt soon turned to anger. "How dare anyone judge me! I am feeding my daughter, taking care of her, and doing what's best for us—how can that possibly be a bad thing? . . . It's gotten to the point now where I am very skeptical about a lot of the so-called 'benefits' of breastfeeding and I get very angry when anyone so much as suggests that my daughter will now somehow be inferior to a child who was nursed." Another woman lamented that although she "can't go a single day without hearing how breast milk is the cure for everything," when she actually attempted breastfeeding, "none of the so-called experts could actually help me solve the problems I was having. So, [I think breastfeeding experts should] spend more time on educating about the *how* and not the *why*. I think we all get the 'why'; it's shoved in my face so much that I actually don't even believe it anymore."

Those who are genuinely interested in finding a more effective form of breastfeeding promotion would be best served by speaking with women like these, who wanted desperately to breastfeed but couldn't. These are the women who see both sides of the argument; the women who have been there, done that, and bought the nursing bra. Just as an anti-tobacco activist might not give the time of day to a smoker's rights group, I fully comprehend why breastfeeding advocates wouldn't care about the feelings of a bunch of disenfranchised breastfeeding "failures." However, if the true goal of breastfeeding advocacy is to promote and support breastfeeding, they *should* care.

"Why not start with asking women what they plan to do, sit down with them before the baby arrives to sketch out whether breastfeeding will work with their lives or not, give them good information on the benefits and challenges of breastfeeding (including unbiased responses on common myths about breastfeeding versus formula feeding that may discourage them wrongly) and its alternatives and then respect the decisions that they make?" suggested a formula-feeding professor of comparative politics when I asked my readers for suggestions on how breastfeeding advocacy could better serve women. "When you go to hospital you should be able to say 'here's what I plan to do' (regarding feeding) and you should be given support accordingly. It's really quite simple at the end of the day—good breastfeeding support respects the woman's right to think and choose for herself within the bounds of basic safety while bad breastfeeding support assumes she needs to be rescued from herself or her own possibly sub-optimal choice." Sara, another mother who "failed" at breastfeeding, wondered "what is so difficult about advocating for something without advocating against other choices by default. Let women make their own informed choices, and help them achieve whatever it is they choose to do."

We also need to be clear on what informed choice *means.* Informed choice means giving women a real-world understanding of what their choice entails. It means offering impartial data on the admittedly better outcomes for breastfed children, but with a clear explanation of what these statistics actually tell us. We shouldn't shy away from sharing facts about the risks of formula feeding, especially in resource-poor countries, but we also can't pretend that the risks of bottle feeding in Zimbabwe are comparable to those in suburban Maryland. The preceding chapters have primarily focused on a specific socioeconomic subset of women; I have only skimmed the surface of the intricacies of formula feeding in the third world. This is partially because I feel these are two entirely different discussions. In order to safely prepare formula, one needs a safe water source—a requirement that is not easily filled in many parts of the world. And there are additional problems inherent in formula feeding in resource-poor areas. Back in 1991, the *Los Angeles Times* reported on formula-related problems in the Ivory Coast,[5] using the frightening example of a middle-class, city-dwelling baby who had become severely ill due to his parents' method of infant feeding. "Six-month-old Jhym had withered away to skin and bone by the time doctors first saw him. The diagnosis: malnutrition caused by improper formula feeding," the article ominously states. "Indiscriminate dumping of large quantities of free or cut-rate powdered baby foods has been an ongoing disaster for babies in the developing world, where many families live without electricity, clean water and refrigeration to easily sanitize and preserve formula. Abidjan is one of the continent's most modern cities, with skyscrapers and six-lane highways, but 30% of the population does not have running water at home. . . . Improperly prepared, mixed with dirty water or over-diluted, formula-feeding can lead to malnutrition, diarrhea, dehydration and death."

Stories like these are used to illustrate the dangers of formula, but often fail to differentiate between the dangers of the formula *itself* and the risks inherent in the act of formula *feeding.* Improving the water supply, for example, could be the takeaway message of these cautionary tales. Approximately 3.5 million people die from water-borne diseases every year, many of whom are past the age of weaning.[6] Though not an easily achievable goal by any means, clean water could improve the health and mortality rates for entire populations, not just infants. "The money it takes to provide water and sanitation services is so small when compared to the payoffs," said one UNICEF official in 2003;[7] this would seem to be a more nuanced solution to child health disparities than simply insisting that all women must breastfeed. The breastfeeding discourse also ignores the fact that not every woman in the developing world lives in a traditional or tribal setting; the same *Los Angeles Times* piece explains that the sick child's parents were choosing formula not because they thought it was better than breastmilk, but because they both *worked.* "Jhym's parents are middle-class white-collar workers. . . . [T]hey left him with his illiterate grandmother so his mother could return to her secretarial job. . . Nurses said the grandmother fed Jhym insufficient amounts of formula and that he lost more than half his body weight before his parents took him to the clinic." What would have prevented Jhym's sickness, according to a representative from a state-run pediatric hospital, was to "persuade working mothers to pump out their breast milk and have baby-sitters feed it to babies with bowls and spoons to avoid the difficulty of having to sanitize feeding bottles and nipples." Although this may indeed solve some formula-related problems, it seems overly simplistic. Informed choice also means providing accurate information about the time and energy breastfeeding may take; the difficulty of combining exclusive breastfeeding and full-time employment; and the physical and psychological problems that can occur while nursing a child. These challenges are not limited to women in affluent nations—they are even more relevant for women living where working and living conditions are subpar at best. Are we really to believe that a secretary living in the Ivory Coast—a country that ranks sixth from the bottom on the 2011 World Economic Forum's gender gap index[8]—will have an employer willing to give her adequate breaks to express milk? And how is she supposed to store the pumped breastmilk without a refrigerator? There is controversy over what is deemed "safe" storage for expressed human milk; according to La Leche League International (LLLI), "There has never been a time when there has been agreement or consensus among health professionals, organizations, government agencies and health ministries, and the research about the storage and handling of human milk."[9] Some guidelines permit pumped milk to be left out at room temperature for up to eight hours,[10] but these same guidelines deem room temperature to be 77 degrees Fahrenheit—a bit chillier than the 90 degree highs (or even the 80 degree norms) of the Ivory Coast. Another study appearing in an African medical journal specifies that in high temperatures like these, breastmilk is safe for only four hours.[11] Powdered formula remains stable until reconstituted with water. If that water is unsafe, the improperly stored breastmilk would obviously still be a better option. But the same developing nations that suffer from unsafe water are typically prone to other third-world problems, and in these environments there may also be dangers in expressing and storing breastmilk—a reality that even LLLI has acknowledged:

> Globally (including within the USA), there are mothers who lack access to freezers, refrigerators, or coolers with blue ice for a long day of work. It is hard to reconcile the possibility of telling mothers who are separated from their infants to discontinue breastfeeding, or at least expressing their milk, and have their infants receive infant formula (possibly prepared incorrectly or in unsanitary conditions or with contaminated water) in questionable environments. . . . The real challenge is trying to find some common ground and common sense between the research and the real life situations around the world in which breastfeeding mothers live and work.

The same document concludes by assuring mothers that breastmilk is *always* better than formula, but then tacks on instructions at the very end about the importance of cleaning pump parts after every use to avoid bacterial contamination.[12] According to the previously mentioned paper on emergency infant feeding in the developed world,[13] formula-feeding parents need to have ample supplies of bottled water to properly clean hands and bottles before prepping formula, because the water supply may be questionable in the wake of a natural disaster. How is a woman supposed to properly clean pump parts in an area of the world where the water supply is *constantly* questionable?

Even within our own country, there seems to be a blatant lack of understanding of the way women live. Low-income women enrolled in the Women, Infants, and Children (WIC) program are heavily inundated with pro-breastfeeding messages. This makes sense on several levels. First, it's to the government's economic advantage if subsidized families decide to breastfeed; formula is expensive, and WIC is Similac's biggest customer. Second, incremental differences in health outcomes are most relevant to those in the toughest circumstances. During the swine flu epidemic of 2009, public health officials noticed that the communities hit hardest with this type of influenza were in poor black and Latino communities; experts claimed that this disparity was due to social factors.[14] If social circumstances can increase the chance of serious health problems or make common illnesses more serious, then even a small improvement in immunity is advantageous for the population most likely to be utilizing WIC.

The criteria that make a woman eligible for WIC may make breastfeeding difficult, however. A 2001 study conducted among WIC participants in New York found that the majority of members were single mothers; it also found that around a quarter of participants worked full time. This probably means a fair percentage of WIC mothers are shouldering the burden of keeping their families afloat; considering that the majority of the WIC demographic is at or below the poverty line and a significant portion hasn't finished high school,[15] much of this income likely comes from non-white-collar employment. I can't imagine trying to pump while working in a factory, for example, or as a migrant farm worker, a waitress, or a childcare provider. (My friend Jen, struggling with her own breastfeeding issues, once asked her nanny if she had nursed her own, now teenage, daughter. The woman looked at her blankly, responding that she had been too busy taking care of someone else's children.) WIC can promote breastfeeding in every way possible (for example, it has incentivized nursing by offering "enhanced food packages" to breastfeeding women and their families, and by allowing nursing mothers to remain in the program longer than their formula-feeding counterparts),[16] but until the program can ensure that women have the familial support and amenable workplace environments that would enable them to pump successfully, we also need to make sure these women are able to formula feed safely and without additional stress. As Christina Bobel, author of the *Paradox of Natural Parenting*, once told me,

> I think we do a lot of our mothering, and make these choices, with a gun to our heads. . . . [I]t's sort of like advising your friend to leave an abusive marriage and she says, well I can't leave him because we have a kid . . . I can't leave because then I'll be destitute. And you want to say, but you deserve better than that. But *you* do not live with the fear of being homeless with children. So you might extract a theoretical sense of what the right thing to do is, but you don't live her life, and so you can't really advise her. You can just tell her that whatever decision she makes you support, because she has to live with the consequences. Of course I would love it if every woman had a fair shot at breastfeeding, a supportive place so that she could do it as long as she wanted. I'd love to live in the world of wish. But until I can personally ensure that's the case for her, I have no business judging her.[17]

I would amend that statement to say that we not only have no business judging her but also have no business blindly promoting breastfeeding to her as a one-size-fits-all "best" solution unless we are prepared to help take care of her other children, subsidize her income, and ensure that she has lactation consultants willing to make free, in-home visits, because if she can't afford a car or gas (lack of transportation and high gas prices were cited in a number of studies as barriers to participating in the WIC program[18] or WIC-related activities,[19] and as reasons for an inability to pick up checks from WIC),[20] how is she going to get to the local WIC office for breastfeeding support?

Not only do the "breast is best" or "breast is normal" memes ignore the lived realities of the specific subset we've focused on in these pages—educated, middle- to upper-income Western women—they are also dismissive of individual women in a variety of situations. The problems surrounding infant feeding for a woman living in the Sahara are quite different from those facing a Manhattanite; the breastfeeding-related problems facing a woman on the Upper West Side of Manhattan may vary from those of a woman in a lower-income area of that same city. And perhaps more important, not all women define motherhood the same way. We are mothers, but not *only* mothers; we are also professionals, wives, sisters, daughters, lovers, friends . . . and yet, women are supposed to happily subjugate these other roles after giving birth. A woman who decides to return to work after several weeks even when offered a longer maternity leave would probably be perceived as cold and "unnatural"; fathers are barely expected to take off work for the delivery. It's not so much a question of women's *rights* as of women's *expectations*—men are able to juggle their various roles (father, professional, husband) while women are assumed to be uniformly affected by biological imperatives and must put "mother" before any other facet of their identities. We can speak of informed choice, but we must also accept that the same "information" might liberate one woman and make another feel imprisoned by her biology.

Informed choice can't mean that we simply hand women a blanket statement of out-of-context facts. All women deserve to be informed about the why, what, and who's of breastfeeding recommendations, in ways they can easily comprehend, without bias or vague, often ignorant notions of cultural or geographic norms. Then, once we have ensured that a woman has received this information, we need to allow her to make her own choices, remembering that *our* own world of wish—however idealistic or well-intentioned—may not necessarily be *hers*.

• • •

There's no doubt that breastfeeding does many wonderful things for many people. Breastfeeding cuts a woman's cancer risk significantly. For children, it can reduce the number of ear infections and gastroenteritis, and has been associated with a lower propensity for obesity and higher IQ. It is a sterile and perfect food, and it can save lives in disaster situations. It allows certain women to heal from childhood sexual trauma by reclaiming their bodies, and affords others a new understanding of what their gender is capable of in the most biological sense. It can be a tremendously rewarding, beautiful experience, which bonds women to their babies in a unique and incomparable way.

There's also no doubt that breastfeeding is a difficult and uncomfortable process for many women. There are other ways to cut cancer risks that don't entail gritting your teeth in pain, or feeling trapped, or desperate, or frustrated. Breastmilk does contain incredible immune-boosting properties, but breastfed kids still get sick, still get ear infections, still get stomach bugs; most bottle-fed children who have access to clean water, good hygiene, and decent healthcare will not suffer long-term effects from having one or two more ear infections or bouts of diarrhea in the first year of their lives, if they get them at all. Breastfeeding can be unbearable for certain women who've suffered from sexual trauma, and can be anything but liberating for women who feel coerced or frightened into doing it. Formula is usually not appropriate in third-world countries, and historically formula companies have done very, very bad things there; but formula also has afforded women a choice, in a nonrhetorical, completely literal sense.

If you breastfeed, your child will most likely thrive. But there will be some small percentage of children who don't get enough milk, who will become dehydrated; there will be some who react terribly to their mother's milk, no matter what she cuts out of her diet.

If you formula feed, your child will most likely thrive. But there will be some small percentage of children who do suffer recurrent ear infections, or get seriously sick from a gastrointestinal infection, or react terribly to all commercial formulas, no matter what type their parents buy.

There will be breastfed kids who are brilliant. There will be formula-fed kids who are brilliant. There will be breastfed kids who get cancer, and formula-fed kids who get cancer. There will be breastfed kids who grow up to be productive, positive members of society, and breastfed kids who end up in prison; formula-fed kids who will be well-adjusted and loving, and formula-fed kids who will become sociopaths.

Mothers who breastfeed will be empowered; mothers who breastfeed will hate nursing and count the days until they can stop. Mothers who formula feed will do so without a second thought; mothers who formula feed will feel guilty and devastated at the loss of the nursing relationship they craved. Mothers will vary in their experiences of motherhood, and babies will be born with different temperaments, physical needs, and circumstances. In order to say that breast is "best," or even "normal," would require qualifying a woman's relationship with her body, with her sexuality, with her sense of self, as "best"; it would require labeling her child as "normal" or "abnormal."

Once, formula feeding reigned supreme as the feeding method of choice. Women were led to mistrust their bodies and to erroneously believe that science knew better than they did. Now, breastfeeding reigns supreme; women are once again being led to mistrust their bodies and to erroneously believe that science knows better than they do.

Perhaps the pendulum swung so far that it ended up in exactly the same place. Perhaps next time it will come to rest a little closer to the middle.

• • •

When my son was a few months old, I had lunch with Nicolle, a woman I'd met during prenatal yoga whose son was born a few weeks before Leo. We began swapping war stories and discovered how similar our experiences had been. It turned out that her son had been tongue-tied and dairy intolerant too. She'd been on an elimination diet, and it had been as difficult for her as it was for me, since we were both vegetarian. Our boys even looked kind of alike, with intense eyes and chalky white skin. It was like we'd been living the same life. Except for one small detail: despite going through much of the same hell that I had, Nicolle was still nursing.

Logic says that I should have found this threatening to my sense of self. I'd been frantically repeating the narrative of *I had no choice but to stop breastfeeding* to myself and anyone who would listen, and here was someone who had been in an eerily similar situation and persevered. What did that say about the truth I held to be self-evident?

But I didn't think twice about it. When I told Nicolle that I had stopped nursing, she looked me straight in the eye and said, "I completely understand. It sounds like you have had a really rough start, but thank god you figured it out and both you and Leo are doing great." That was it. No pity, no suggestions, and not one iota of judgment came from her lips, even though she of all people had every right to judge me. It was as if she hadn't even considered the fact that our situations were parallel. We had two separate stories, two separate experiences, and two separate babies, no matter how alike all of these might appear on paper.

As the conversation progressed, she told me how much breastfeeding meant to her, and how relieved she felt that she could still do it despite her son's allergies. That didn't mean the necessary elimination diet didn't stink, but it was worth it to her, because she loved nursing her child. I told her that Leo and I had never quite gotten the hang of nursing; that breastfeeding had been inexplicably intertwined with my postpartum depression,.so for me it had been no loss to quit. And then we stopped talking about how and what we fed our kids and moved on to more important topics, like the daunting prospect of postpartum sex and the push-pull of going back to work.

Eventually, we had to interrupt the conversation because both babies started wailing. Nicolle lifted her shirt and I pulled out my bottle, and we both fed our children in the best way we could. As if these things were just preferences. Which is, of course, exactly what they should be.

NOTES

INTRODUCTION

1. Center for Parenting Culture Studies 2011.
2. Feldman et al. 2009.

1. PRECONCEIVED NOTIONS

1. Centers for Disease Control and Prevention 2011.
2. Thompson 1998; quotation from Graff 2007.
3. Hey Facebook, Breastfeeding Is Not Obscene (Facebook group page), Question for the formula feeder, www.facebook.com/topic.php?uid=2517126532&topic=8697 (accessed May 2009).
4. World Health Organization 1981.
5. Solomon 1981.
6. Velasquez 1992, pp. 304–312.
7. Blum 1999; Hausman 2003; Palmer 2009.
8. UNICEF 1990.
9. Palmer 2009.
10. Breastfeeding Task Force of Greater Los Angeles, The risks of infant formula, www.breastfeedingtaskforla.org/resources/ABMRisks.htm (accessed September 2010). The authors then cite a 2007 Agency

for Healthcare Research and Quality (AHRQ) report as evidence of these risks. The summary statement of that document conservatively assesses that, although the report shows a reduced risk of numerous ailments in developed countries related to breastfeeding, "because almost all the data in this review were gathered from observational studies, one should not infer causality based on these findings. Also, there is a wide range of quality of the body of evidence across different health outcomes. For future studies, clear subject selection criteria and definition of 'exclusive breastfeeding,' reliable collection of feeding data, controlling for important confounders including child-specific factors, and blinded assessment of the outcome measures will help" (Tufts–New England Medical Center Evidence-Based Practice Center 2007). I have seen the AHRQ report manipulated every which way to support dramatic claims about the "risks" of formula feeding, but those who reference it usually neglect to mention the strong caveats attached to the data.

11. O'Connor 1998.

12. Centers for Disease Control and Prevention 2010a.

13. Wiessinger 1996.

14. Toronto Public Health 2010.

15. Ban the Bags, Broad coalition opposes formula marketing, http://banthebags.org/24 (accessed October 9, 2009).

16. Bisphenol A, a chemical found in plastic bottles.

17. Granju 2004.

18. Granju 2004.

19. Kukla 2006, p. 174.

20. Morales 2003.

21. Biancuzzo 2001.

22. American Academy of Pediatrics, Section on Breastfeeding 2005. Shortly before this book went to press, the AAP released an updated statement that used even stronger language, claiming that breastfeeding "should not be considered a lifestyle choice but rather a public health issue" due to "evidence-based studies" that had "confirmed and quantitated the risks of not breastfeeding" (American Academy of Pediatrics, Section on Breastfeeding 2012).

23. Granju 2004.

24. Granju 2004.

25. American Academy of Pediatrics, Children's health topics—Breastfeeding, www.aap.org/healthtopics/breastfeeding.cfm (accessed May 1, 2010).

26. Schanler, O'Connor, and Lawrence 1999.

27. Barclay 2008.

28. Dworkin 2002a.

29. Dworkin 2010.

30. O'Mara 2004.

31. Murphy 2010.

32. Lauwers and Swisher 2005, p. 53.

33. Knaak 2010.

34. Newman 2000.

2. LACTATION FAILURES

1. Rosin 2009.

2. Brace 2007.

3. Blum 1999; Golden 2001.

4. Blum 1999.

5. Apple 1987.

6. Blum 1999.

7. Blum 1999, p. 31.

8. The Unnecesarean, www.theunnecesarean.com/ (accessed January 2011).

9. Hausman 2010, pp. 21–22.

10. Wells 2006.

11. Wells 2006.

12. Maushart 2000, pp. 151–152.

13. Hrdy 2009.

14. Alvarez 2003.

15. Haggvist et al. 2010.

16. Could Norway's impressive breastfeeding rates be made possible by the fact that Norwegian women are finding ways to "take the edge off" with the use of supplements? A 2002 study even found that women who engaged in some bottle feeding between four and twelve

weeks postpartum were 98 percent less likely to stop breastfeeding than those who exclusively nursed. Schwartz et al. 2002.

17. Best for Babes, www.bestforbabes.org (accessed February 2010).

18. Golden 2001.

19. Wells 2006, p. 41.

20. KellyMom.com, Average weight gain for breastfed babies, http://kellymom.com/bf/normal/weight-gain/ (accessed April 2012).

21. Baby-Friendly USA, www.babyfriendlyusa.org (accessed July 2010).

22. Academy of Breastfeeding Medicine 2009a.

23. San Diego Breastfeeding Coalition, www.breastfeeding.org/bfacts/bottle.html (accessed October 2008).

24. Children's Hospital Boston, What is necrotizing enterocolitis? www.childrenshospital.org/az/Site1336/mainpageS1336P0.html (accessed February 2011).

25. Katz et al. 2010.

26. Dimity McDowell, Is nipple confusion a myth? www.parenting.com/article/is-nipple-confusion-a-myth? (accessed August 2010).

27. Greenberg 1999.

28. Moritz 2010.

29. Moritz et al. 2005.

30. Moritz 2010.

31. Moritz 2010.

32. Taffy Brodesser-Akner, The breastfeeding conspiracy, www.babble.com/baby/baby-feeding-nutrition/breastfeeding-problems-low-breast-milk-supply-lactation-consultant/ (accessed January 2011).

33. Neifert et al. 1990.

34. Stuebe 2010.

35. FamilyStuff.com 2009.

36. Alvarez 2003.

37. Haggvist et al. 2010.

38. Chin 2010.

39. Pontifical Academy of Sciences and the Royal Society Working Group 1995. Prentice's remarks are posted online at http://archive.unu.edu/unupress/food/8F174e/8F174E04.htm.

40. Horvath 2009.

41. World Health Organization 2010.

42. AVERT, AIDS charity AVERT, www.avert.org/aids-hiv-charity-avert.htm (accessed September 2011).

43. AVERT, AIDS charity AVERT, www.avert.org/aids-hiv-charity-avert.htm (accessed September 2011).

44. Read and the Committee on Pediatric AIDS 2003.

45. Isolauri et al. 1999

46. Isolauri et al. 1999.

47. Schulmeister et al. 2007.

48. LiveScience 2010.

49. David Galbraith, Human biomonitoring—An overview, Galbraith Biomonitoring Notes, www.isrtp.org/nonmembers/Human%20Biomonitoring%206–05/Galbraith%20Biomon%20Notes.pdf (accessed November 2010).

50. Centers for Disease Control and Prevention 2010b.

51. Gross-Loh 2004.

52. World Health Organization 1981, article 6.

53. World Health Organization 1981, article 4.

54. Lakshman, Ogilvie, and Ong 2009.

55. Lee and Furedi 2005.

56. William Sears, Bottle feeding, Ask Dr. Sears, www.askdrsears.com/html/0/T000100.asp (accessed October 2010).

57. Associated Press 2011.

58. U.K. Department of Health, Food Standards Agency, Guidance for health professionals on safe preparation, storage and handling of powdered infant formula, www.food.gov.uk/multimedia/pdfs/formulaguidance.pdf.

59. Mennella, Ventura, and Beauchamp 2011.

60. Osborn and Sinn 2003.

3. OF HUMAN BONDING

1. Kleiman 2010.
2. Kohen 2005.
3. Marks and Spatz 2003.
4. Marks and Spatz 2003.

5. Marks and Spatz 2003.

6. Newman 1997.

7. Julie Mennella, Alcohol's effect on lactation, National Institute on Alcohol Abuse and Alcoholism, http://pubs.niaaa.nih.gov/publications/arh25–3/230–234.htm (accessed November 2010).

8. Anderson et al. 2007.

9. Hale 2010.

10. Hale 2002.

11. Kohen 2005.

12. Academy of Breastfeeding Medicine Protocol Committee 2008.

13. Black and Hill 2003.

14. Gallup et al. 2010.

15. Nelson 2009.

16. Harutyunyan 2009.

17. Rochman 2011.

18. IBCLC: Pathways, http://americas.iblce.org/exam-eligibility-pathways (accessed September 2010).

19. Lauwers and Swisher 2005, p. 80.

20. Sonkin 2005.

21. Jansen, Weerth, and Riksen-Walraven 2008.

22. Britton, Britton, and Gronwaldt 2006.

23. Jansen, Weerth, and Riksen-Walraven 2008, p. 505.

24. Knaak 2010.

25. Fearless Formula Feeder 2010c.

26. Leon 1998.

27. Fearless Formula Feeder 2010a.

28. Jansen, Weerth, and Riksen-Walraven 2008, p. 510.

29. Fairlie, Gillman, and Rich-Edwards 2009.

30. McCarthy 2007.

31. Renfrew Center Foundation for Eating Disorders 2002, revised 2003.

32. Foster, Slade, and Wilson 1996.

33. Stapleton, Fielder, and Kirkham 2008.

34. Stapleton, Fielder, and Kirkham 2008.

35. Stapleton, Fielder, and Kirkham 2008, p. 112.

4. THE DAIRY QUEENS

1. U.S. Census Bureau 2008; U.S. Department of Labor, Bureau of Labor Statistics 2011.

2. Lepore 2009.

3. World Health Organization, Exclusive breastfeeding, www.who.int/nutrition/topics/exclusive_breastfeeding/en/ (accessed March 2011).

4. Li, Fein, and Grummer-Strawn 2010.

5. Hanna et al. 2004.

6. Lawrence 1999.

7. Medela, Pump-in-Style advanced on-the-go tote, www.medelabreastfeedingus.com/products/breast-pumps/551/pump-in-style-advanced---on-the-go-tote (accessed September 2010); Medela promotional pop-up ad, received by the author from Babycenter.com, October 2010.

8. Ohlemacher 2010.

9. 061009 Breastfeeding Promotion Act, June 10, 2009, website of U.S. Representative Carolyn Maloney, http://maloney.house.gov/documents/women/breastfeeding/061009%20Breastfeeding%20Promotion%20Act.pdf (accessed August 2010).

10. Rippeyoung and Noonan 2010.

11. Granju 1998.

12. Jacknowitz 2004.

13. Rippeyoung and Noonan 2010.

14. Hochschild and Machung 1989.

15. Bentovim 2002.

16. Bentovim 2010.

17. Bentovim 2002, p. 9.

18. U.S. Department of Labor, Wage and Hour Division 2010.

19. Gane-McCalla 2011.

20. Drago, Hayes, and Yi 2010.

21. Rippeyoung and Noonan 2010.

22. Baker and Milligan 2007.

23. Noonan 2011.

24. Bentovim 2010.

25. Rippeyoung and Noonan 2010.

26. Young 2009.

27. Jacknowitz 2004.

28. Bobel 2010.

29. Bobel 2010.

30. Blum 2010.

31. Penny Van Esterik, Breastfeeding: A feminist issue, World Alliance for Breastfeeding Action, www.waba.org.my/resources/activitysheet/acsh4.htm (accessed March 2012).

32. National Organization for Women, Info about NOW, www.now.org/organization/info.html (accessed August 2010).

33. Galtry 2000.

34. Dettwyler 2009.

35. Dettwyler 2009.

36. H. E. Baber, Liberal feminism, n.d., University of California, San Diego, http://home.sandiego.edu/~baber/research/liberalfeminism.pdf (accessed September 2010).

37. Rippeyoung and Noonan 2010.

38. Oakley 2010.

39. Rippeyoung 2011.

40. Barston and Heisler 2010.

41. Barston and Heisler 2010.

42. Smith 2008.

43. Petosa 1998.

44. Boteach 2006.

45. Symposia on Breastfeeding and Feminism 2011.

46. Third Annual Symposium on Breastfeeding and Feminism: Proceedings 2008.

47. UNICEF, Unicef in action—The International Code, www.unicef.org/programme/breastfeeding/code.htm (accessed September 2010).

48. Gorenstein quoted in Layne, Vostral, and Boyer 2010, pp. 18–19.

49. Valenti 2011.

50. Feminist Breeder 2011.

51. Rebel Raising 2011.

52. Williams 2010, p. 108.

5. DAMN LIES AND STATISTICS

1. American Academy of Pediatrics, Section on Breastfeeding 2005.

2. STATS, About STATS, http://stats.org/about.htm (accessed October 2010).

3. Goldin, Smyth, and Foulkes 2006.

4. Goldin 2009b.

5. Pontifical Academy of Sciences and the Royal Society Working Group 1995, discussion of paper by Howie.

6. Evenhouse and Reilly 2005.

7. Evenhouse and Reilly 2010.

8. Evenhouse and Reilly 2010.

9. Goldin 2009a.

10. This quotation is often attributed to Mark Twain, but he attributed it to Benjamin Disraeli; others cite Sir Charles Wentworth Dilke, Leonard H. Courtney, and others.

11. Crowther, Reynolds, and Tansey 2007, pp. 81–82.

12. Last 2002.

13. Law 2000.

14. Fildes 1989.

15. Law 2010.

16. Law 2000, pp. 413–414.

17. Wolf 2010a.

18. Wolf 2010b.

19. Wolf 2010b.

20. Daily Mail Reporter 2011.

21. Tufts–New England Medical Center Evidence-Based Practice Center 2007.

22. U.S. Department of Health and Human Services 2011.

23. Butte 2001.

24. Li, Parsons, and Power 2003.

25. Kramer et al. 2001.

26. Piotrowski 2009.
27. Chin and Solomonik 2009.
28. Science Daily 2008.
29. Moore 2010.
30. Shelton 2009.
31. Good Morning America, Fat babies: Parents put fat babies on diet, http://abcnews.go.com/GMA/fat-babies-parents-put-fat-babies-diet/story?id=12216642&page=3 (accessed October 2010).
32. The Nurses' Health Study, www.channing.harvard.edu/nhs/ (accessed January 2011).
33. Stuebe et al. 2005.
34. Stuebe et al. 2009.
35. Troy et al. 1996.
36. Weiten 2008.
37. Taubes 2008.
38. Kolata 2009.
39. Stenson 2003.
40. Melville 2010.
41. Mayo Clinic Staff 2011.
42. Doughty 2011.
43. Wrotniak et al. 2008.
44. Law 2010.
45. Wolf 2010a, p. 35.
46. Bartick and Reinhold 2010.
47. CBS News/AP 2009.
48. Falco 2009.
49. Falco 2009.
50. Palumbo 2011.
51. Tufts–New England Medical Center Evidence-Based Practice Center 2007.
52. Palumbo 2011.
53. Brownstein 2009.
54. Blacktating Blog 2009.
55. Forbes 2009.
56. Wolf 2010b.

6. SOOTHING THE SAVAGE BREAST

1. PhD in Parenting 2010b.

2. These are available online or in stores from Similac, Enfamil, and Nestlé Good Start, in a variety of sizes.

3. McGuiness-Snider 2011.

4. Eickemeyer 2011.

5. Faul 1991.

6. Water.org, One billion affected, http://water.org/learn-about-the-water-crisis/billion/ (accessed November 18, 2011).

7. UNICEF Press Centre 2003.

8. Hausmann, Tyson, and Zahidi 2011.

9. Crase and Furr 2008.

10. Eglash 2004.

11. Igumbor et al. 2000.

12. Crase and Furr 2008.

13. Gribble and Berry 2011.

14. Knox 2009.

15. Connor et al. 2010.

16. U.S. Department of Agriculture, Food and Nutrition Service 2011.

17. Bobel 2010.

18. Chee and McCloskey 2006; New York State Department of Health, Division of Nutrition, Evaluation and Analysis Unit 2011.

19. Damron et al. 1999.

20. Rosenberg, Alperen, and Chiasson 2003.

REFERENCES AND FURTHER READING

Academy of Breastfeeding Medicine. 2009a. ABM clinical protocol #3: Hospital guidelines for the use of supplementary feedings in the healthy term neonate, revised 2009. *Breastfeeding Medicine* 4 (3): 175–178.

———. 2009b. First annual summit on breastfeeding. *Breastfeeding Medicine* 4 (s1): S1–S86.

Academy of Breastfeeding Medicine Advocacy Committee. 2008. ABM Advocacy Committee response to NPR broadcast. www.bfmed.org/Media/Files/Documents/pdf/Press%20Releases/4-2008%20ABM%20Advocacy%20Committee%20Response%20to%20NPR%20Broadcast.pdf (accessed September 2011).

Academy of Breastfeeding Medicine Protocol Committee. 2008. ABM clinical protocol #18: Use of antidepressants in nursing mothers. *Breastfeeding Medicine* 3 (1): 44–52.

Allen, Greg. 2009. Shapely science-distorting lactivists annoy pump-hating, stressed-out, guilt-ridden, haranguing shrew. DaddyTypes.com. March 15. http://daddytypes.com/2009/03/15/shapely_science-distorting_lactivists_annoy_pump-hating_stressed-out_guilt-ridden_haranguing_shrew.php (accessed October 2010).

Allen, Lindsay H. 1994. Maternal micronutrient malnutrition: Effects on breast milk and infant nutrition, and priorities for intervention. *SCN News—Maternal and Child Nutrition*, no. 11: 29–33.

Alvarez, Lizette. 2003. Norway leads industrial nations back to breastfeeding. *New York Times*, October 21.

American Academy of Pediatrics. 2002. *American Academy of Pediatrics new mother's guide to breastfeeding*. Edited by Joan Younger Meek and Sherill Tippens. New York: Bantam Books.

American Academy of Pediatrics, Section on Breastfeeding. 2005. Breastfeeding and the use of human milk. *Pediatrics* 115 (2): 496–506.

———. 2012. Breastfeeding and the use of human milk. *Pediatrics* 129 (3): e827–e841. Originally published online February 27, DOI: 10.1542/peds.2011–3552.

American Pregnancy Association. 2007. Miscarriage. July. www.americanpregnancy.org/pregnancycomplications/miscarriage.html (accessed April 2011).

Anderson, A. K., D. M. McDougald, and M. Steiner-Asiedu. 2010. Dietary trans fatty acid intake and maternal and infant adiposity. *European Journal of Clinical Nutrition* 64:1308–1315.

Anderson, Philip O., Jason B. Sauberan, James R. Lane, and Steven S. Rossi. 2007. Hydrocodone excretion into breast milk: The first two reported cases. *Breastfeeding Medicine* 2 (1): 10–14.

Anonymous. 2006. Slate Dr.: Breast is best? Or just so-so? March 30. http://daddytypes.com/2006/03/30/slate_dr_breast_is_best_or_just_so-so.php (accessed September 25, 2011).

Apple, Rima Dombrow. 1987. *Mothers and medicine: A social history of infant feeding, 1890–1950*. Madison: University of Wisconsin Press.

Artis, Julie. 2009. Breastfeed at your own risk. Fall. http://contexts.org/articles/fall-2009/breastfeed-at-your-own-risk/ (accessed November 2009).

———. 2010. Interview with the author. Chicago, July 26.

Arvola, T., and D. Holmberg-Marttila. 1999. Benefits and risks of elimination diets. *Annals of Medicine* 31 (4): 293–298.

Arvola, T., J. Hvitfelt-Koskelainen, U.-M. Eriksson, and A. Tahvanainen. 2000. Correspondence—Breastfeeding and allergy counselling: Theory and practice. *Acta Pædiatrica* 89:365–374.

Associated Press. 2011. Wal-Mart pulls formula after Mo. baby's death. December 11. http://news.yahoo.com/wal-mart-pulls-formula-mo-babys-death-014357466.html.

Baber, H. E. 2010. Telephone interview with the author. October 28.

Babycenter.com Message Board. 2009. Guilt and persecution: Formula feeding vs. breastfeeding—The debate team. January 6. http://community.babycenter.com/post/a4002535/guilt_and_persecution_formula_feeding_vs._breast?intcmp=Rel_SP_post (accessed February 2009).

Baby-Friendly USA. 2011. 105 U.S. baby friendly hospitals as of January 27, 2011. www.babyfriendlyusa.org/eng/03.html (accessed February 2011).

Baker, Michael, and Kevin S. Milligan. 2007. Maternal employment, breastfeeding, and health: Evidence from maternity leave mandates. Working paper, National Bureau of Economic Research. www.nber.org/papers/w13188.

Balint, Peter. 2009. Should the promotion of breastfeeding be government policy? Australian Political Science Association. Canberra, Australia.

Barclay, Laurie. 2008. Pediatrician promotion of breast-feeding among their patients has declined. *Archives of Pediatrics and Adolescent Medicine* 162:1142–1149.

Barnes, J., A. Stein, T. Smith, and J. I. Pollock. 1997. Extreme attitudes to body shape, social and psychological factors and a reluctance to breastfeed. *Journal of the Royal Society of Medicine* 90:552–559.

Barston, Suzanne, and Christian Heisler. 2010. FFF Friday: A dad's two cents. October 15. http://fearlessformulafeeder.blogspot.com/2010/10/fff-friday-dads-two-cents.html (accessed March 2011).

Bartick, Melissa. 2007. Making the case: Effective language for breastfeeding advocacy. Massachusetts Breastfeeding Coalition. March. http://massbfc.org/advocacy/makeCase.html (accessed August 2009).

Bartick, Melissa, and Arnold Reinhold. 2010. The burden of suboptimal breastfeeding in the United States: A pediatric cost analysis. *Pediatrics.* April 5. http://pediatrics.aappublications.org/content/early/2010/04/05/peds.2009–1616.full.pdf+html (accessed March 2012).

Bartlett, Alison. 2005. *Breastwork: Rethinking breastfeeding.* Sydney, Australia: University of New South Wales Press.

BBC News. 2010. Scrap "breast is best" slogan, say campaigners. June 21. www.bbc.co.uk/news/10368037 (accessed June 22, 2010).

Bentovim, Orit Avishai. 2002. Family-friendly as a double-edged sword: Lesson from the "lactation-friendly" workplace. Working Paper no. 46, Center for Working Families, University of California, Berkeley.

———. 2010. Telephone interview with the author. October 9.

Biancuzzo, Marie. 2001. Not just a slogan; Breast *is* best! *Breastfeeding Outlook*, issue 2. www.breastfeedingoutlook.com/documents/editorials/2001.2-BreastIsBest.pdf.

Black, Ronald A., and D. Ashley Hill. 2003. Over the counter medications in pregnancy. *American Family Physician* 67 (12): 2517–2524.

Blacktating Blog. 2009. Study: Lack of breastfeeding costs lives, billions of dollars. April 5. www.blacktating.com/2010/04/study-lack-of-breastfeeding-costs-lives.html (accessed April 6, 2009).

Block, Jennifer. 2010. Ina May Gaskin: The mother of midwifery on the "lost art" of breastfeeding. www.babble.com/baby/baby-feeding-nutrition/ina-may-gaskin-midwifery-natural-childbirth-breastfeeding/ (accessed January 2011).

Blum, Linda. 1999. *At the breast: Ideologies of breastfeeding and motherhood in the United States.* Boston: Beacon Press.

———. 2010. Interview with the author. Arlington, MA, August 3.

Bobel, Christina. 2001a. Bounded liberation: A focused study of La Leche League International. *Gender and Society* 15 (1): 130–151.

———. 2001b. *The paradox of natural mothering.* Philadelphia: Temple University Press.

———. 2010. Interview with the author. Arlington, MA, August 3.

Bogen, Debra L., Barbara H. Hanusa, and Robert C. Whitaker. 2004. The effect of breast-feeding with and without formula use on the risk of obesity at 4 years of age. *Obesity Research* 12:1527–1535.

Bonyata, Kelly. 2002. Is my exclusively breastfed baby gaining too much weight? October 24. www.kellymom.com/babyconcerns/growth/weight-toomuch.html (accessed September 2010).

Boseley, Sarah. 2010. Bottle-feeding babies can lead to adult obesity. September 20. www.guardian.co.uk/lifeandstyle/2010/sep/30/bottle-feeding-babies-adult-obesity (accessed September 2010).

Boteach, Rabbi Shmuley. 2006. Moms, don't forget to feed your marriages. BeliefNet. July. www.beliefnet.com/Love-Family/

Relationships/2006/07/Moms-Dont-Forget-To-Feed-Your-Marriages.aspx?p = 1 (accessed September 2010).

Boyer, Kate, and Maia Boswell-Penc. 2010. Breast pumps: A feminist technology, or (yet) "more work for mother"? In *Feminist technology*, edited by Linda Layne, Sharra Vostral, and Kate Boyer, 119–135. Urbana: University of Illinois Press.

Brace, Laura. 2007. Rousseau, maternity and the politics of emptiness (Jean-Jacques Rousseau). *Polity* 39 (July): 361–383.

Britton, Cathryn. 2003. Breastfeeding: A natural phenomenon or a cultural construct? In *The Social Context of Birth*, edited by Catherine Squire, 305–317. Milton Keynes, United Kingdom: Radcliffe Publishing.

Britton, John R., Helen L. Britton, and Virginia Gronwaldt. 2006. Breastfeeding, sensitivity, and attachment. *Pediatrics* 118 (5): e1436–e1443 .

Brownstein, Joseph. 2009. Breastfeeding may save U.S. $13 billion per year. ABC News. April 5. http://abcnews.go.com/Health/breast feeding-failure-costs-us-billion-year/story?id=10272015&page=2 (accessed April 6, 2009).

Butler, Rebecca. 2009. Breastfeeding and the fast-gaining baby. October 14. www.llli.org/llleaderweb/lv/lvjulaugsep06p54.html (accessed October 2010).

Butte, N. F. 2001. The role of breastfeeding in obesity. *Pediatric Clinics of North America* 48 (1): 189–198.

Butterworth, Trevor. 2010. The wrongs of righteous research. December 3. http://blogs.forbes.com/trevorbutterworth/2010/12/03/the-wrongs-of-righteous-research/ (accessed December 3, 2010).

Cannold, Leslie. 2008. Breastfeeding: Differing advice flows oh so freely. January 27. http://cannold.com/articles/article/breastfeed ing-differing-advice-flows-oh-so-freely/ (accessed January 2011).

CBS News/AP. 2009. More breastfeeding could save 900 babies a year. CBS News. April 5. www.cbsnews.com/stories/2010/04/05/health/main6364292.shtml (accessed April 6, 2009).

Center for Parenting Culture Studies. 2011. About CPCS. May 4. http://blogs.kent.ac.uk/parentingculturestudies/about/ (accessed November 20, 2011).

Centers for Disease Control and Prevention. 2010a. Breastfeeding report card. www.cdc.gov/breastfeeding/data/reportcard2.htm.

———. 2010b. National biomonitoring program. March 12. www.cdc.gov/biomonitoring (accessed February 2011).

———. 2011. Breastfeeding among U.S. children born 2000–2008. CDC National Immunization Survey. www.cdc.gov/breastfeeding/data/NIS_data/ (accessed April 2012).

Chalmers B., Levitt C., Heaman M., O'Brien B., Sauve R., Kaczorowski J. 2009. Breastfeeding rates and hospital breastfeeding practices in Canada: A national survey of women. *Birth* 36 (2): 122–132.

Chee, Joanne, and Melvatha McCloskey. 2006. An ethnographic study of the factors affecting the nutritional patterns of Navajo women and their children in the WIC program. Paper, USDA Small Grants Program and American Indian Studies Program, University of Arizona.

Chin, Nancy P. 2010. Environmental toxins: Physical, social, and emotional. *Breastfeeding Medicine* 5 (5): 223–224.

Chin, Nancy P., and Anna Solomonik. 2009. Inadequate: A metaphor for the lives of low-income women? *Breastfeeding Medicine* 4 (S1): S41–S43.

Connor, Patty, Susan Bartlett, Michele Mendelson, Katherine Condon, James Sutcliffe, et al. 2010. *WIC participant and program characteristics 2008, WIC-08-PC.* Alexandria, VA: U.S. Department of Agriculture, Food and Nutrition Service, Office of Research and Analysis, WIC.

Coulter, R. H., and M. B. Pinto. 1995. Guilt appeals in advertising: What are their effects? *Journal of Applied Psychology* 80 (6): 697–705.

Cox, Lauren. 2009. Are some breastfeeding claims overblown? ABC.com. April 27. http://abcnews.go.com/print?id=7424844 (accessed May 2009).

Crase, Betty, and Sara Dodder Furr. 2008. LLLI revises milk storage guidelines. *Leaven* 44 (3): 2–4.

Crenshaw, Jeanette. 2009. Care practice #6. July. www.lamaze.org/ChildbirthEducators/ResourcesforEducators/CarePracticePapers/NoSeparation/tabid/488/Default.aspx (accessed March 22, 2010).

Crossley, Michele L. 2009. Breastfeeding as a moral imperative: An autoethnographic study. *Feminism and Psychology* 19 (1): 71–87.

Crowther, S. M., L. A. Reynolds, and E. M. Tansey. 2007. *The resurgence of breastfeeding, 1975–2000: The transcript of a Witness Seminar held by the Wellcome Trust Centre.* London: Wellcome Trust Centre.

Daily Mail Reporter. 2011. Michelle Obama backs breastfeeding in workplace to cut down on obesity. Mail Online. February 16. www.dailymail.co.uk/news/article-1357345/Michelle-Obama-backs-breastfeeding-workplace-cut-obesity.html#ixzz1EiaQ8g1B (accessed February 17, 2011).

Damron, D., P. Langenberg, J. Anliker, M. Ballesteros, R. Feldman, and S. Havas. 1999. Factors associated with attendance in a voluntary nutrition education program. *American Journal of Health Promotion* 13 (5): 268–275.

Dennis, C. L., and K. McQueen. 2009. The relationship between infant-feeding outcomes and postpartum depression: A qualitative systematic review. *Pediatrics* 123 (4): e736–e751.

Department of Health and Human Services. 2010. HHS blueprints and breastfeeding policy statements. WomensHealth.gov. 2010. www.womenshealth.gov/breastfeeding/government-programs/hhs-blueprints-and-policy-statements/ (accessed September 2010).

Der, Geoff, G. David Batty, and Ian J. Deary. 2006. Effect of breast feeding on intelligence in children: Prospective study, sibling pairs analysis, and meta-analysis. *British Medical Journal,* October: Online First.

Dettwyler, Katherine A. 2009. Is breastfeeding advocacy anti-feminist? An essay by Katherine A. Dettwyler. July 19. www.lactivistleanings.com/education/is-breastfeeding-advocacy-anti-feminist-an-essay-by-katherine-a-dettwyler/ (accessed October 2010).

Dewey, Kathryn G., Laurie A. Nommsen-Rivers, M. Jane Heinig, and Roberta J. Cohen. 2003. Risk factors for suboptimal infant breastfeeding behavior, delayed onset of lactation, and excess neonatal weight loss. *Pediatrics* 112 (3): 607–619.

Dewey, K. G. 2001. Maternal and fetal stress are associated with impaired lactogenesis in humans. *Journal of Nutrition* 131 (11): 3012S–3015S .

Doughty, Steve. 2011. Working mothers risk damaging their child's prospects. *Daily Mail,* November 4. www.dailymail.co.uk/news/article-30342/Working-mothers-risk-damaging-childs-prospects.html.

Drago, Robert, Jeffrey Hayes, and Youngmin Yi. 2010. *Better health for mothers and children: Breastfeeding accommodations under the Affordable Care Act.* Washington, DC: Institute of Women's Policy Research.

Dworkin, Barry. 2002a. The hazards of breastfeeding. *Ottawa Citizen,* January 8.

———. 2002b. The hazards of discussing breastfeeding. *Ottawa Citizen,* January 15.

———. 2010. Telephone interview with the author. August 10.

Edwards, Stassa. 2010. Will Elisabeth Badinter's new book rile Oprah mommies? MsMagazine.com. July 16. http://msmagazine.com/blog/blog/2010/07/16/will-elisabeth-badinters-new-book-rile-oprah-mommies/ (accessed November 1, 2011).

Eglash, Anne. 2004. *Protocol #8: Human milk storage information for home use for healthy full-term infants.* New Rochelle, NY: Academy of Breastfeeding Medicine.

Eickemeyer, Suchada. 2011. 4 reasons the breastmilk/formula debate makes me want to pull my hair out. MamaEve.com. January 30. www.mamaeve.com/caring-for-baby-a-toddler/breastfeeding/257–4-reasons-the-breastmilkformula-debate-makes-me-want-to-pull-my-hair-out/ (accessed January 30, 2011).

Emmet, Pauline M., and Imogen S. Rogers. 1997. Properties of human milk and their relationship with maternal nutrition. *Early Human Development* 49 (supp. 1): S7–S28.

Eriksen, Thomas Hylland. 1993. Being Norwegian in a shrinking world: Reflections on Norwegian identity. In *Continuity and change: Aspects of modern Norway,* edited by Anne Cohen Kiel, 11–37. Oslo: Scandinavian University Press.

Erlanger, Stephen. 2010. Elisabeth Badinter defends the imperfect mother. *New York Times,* June 4. www.nytimes.com/2010/06/06/fashion/06Culture.html?pagewanted = all.

Evenhouse, Eirik, and Siobhan Reilly. 2005. Improved estimates of the benefits of breastfeeding using sibling comparisons to reduce selection bias. *Health Services Research* 40 (6, part 1): 1781–1802.

———. 2010. Telephone interview with the author. October 22.

Faircloth, Charlotte. 2010. "What science says is best": Parenting practices, scientific authority and maternal identity. *Sociological Research Online* 15 (4). www.socresonline.org.uk/15/4/4.html.

Fairlie, Tarayn G., Matthew W. Gillman, and Janet Rich-Edwards. 2009. High pregnancy-related anxiety and prenatal depressive symptoms as predictors of intention to breastfeed and breastfeeding initiation. *Journal of Women's Health (Larchmont)* 18 (7): 945–953.

Falceto, Olga Garcia, Elsa R. J. Giugliani, and Carmen Luiza C. Fernandes. 2004. Influence of parental mental health on early termination of breast-feeding: A case-control study. *Journal of the American Board of Family Medicine* 17 (3): 173–183.

Falco, Miriam. 2009. Study: Lack of breastfeeding costs lives, billions of dollars. CNN.com. April 5. http://articles.cnn.com/2010–04–05/health/breastfeeding.costs_1_breastfeeding-sudden-infant-death-syndrome-preterm-babies?_s = PM:HEALTH (accessed April 6, 2009).

FamilyStuff.com. 2009. Breastfeeding myths debunked. October 16. www.familystuff.com/2009/10/16/breasfeeding-myths-debunked (accessed July 2010).

Faul, Michelle. 1991. Improper formula feeding spreads malnutrition, death in third world babies. *Los Angeles Times,* May 19. http://articles.latimes.com/1991–05–19/news/mn-2981_1_formula-feed.

Fearless Formula Feeder. 2010a. FFF Friday: I had to redefine what it meant to be a good mother. Fearless Formula Feeder. October. http://fearlessformulafeeder.blogspot.com/2010/10/fff-friday-i-had-to-redefine-what-it.html (accessed October 2010).

———. 2010b. FFF Friday: That was the moment I refused to listen to everybody but myself. Fearless Formula Feeder. July 2. http://fearlessformulafeeder.blogspot.com/2010/07/fff-friday-that-was-moment-i-refused-to.html (accessed July 2, 2010).

———. 2010c. FFF Friday: This is but a small moment. Fearless Formula Feeder. November. http://fearlessformulafeeder.blogspot.com/2010/11/fff-friday-this-is-but-small-moment.html (accessed November 2010).

———. 2011. Formula feeding in disaster situations: Is there a dose of reality in your emergency kit? Fearless Formula Feeder. November

9. www.fearlessformulafeeder.com/2011/11/formula-feeding-in-disaster-situations.html (accessed November 20, 2011).

Feldman, Ruth, Adi Granat, Clara Pariente, Hannah Kanety, Jacob Kuint, and Eva Gilboa-Schechtman. 2009. Maternal depression and anxiety across the postpartum year and infant social engagement, fear regulation, and stress reactivity. *Journal of the American Academy of Child and Adolescent Psychiatry* 48 (9): 919–927.

Feminist Breeder. 2011. You think women aren't vulnerable to marketing? Check your privilege. October 6. http://thefeministbreeder.com/you-think-women-arent-vulnerable-to-marketing-check-your-privilege/ (accessed October 7, 2011).

Fewtrell, Mary, David C. Wilson, Ian Booth, and Alan Lucas. 2011. Six months of exclusive breast feeding: How good is the evidence? *British Medical Journal* 342:c5955.

Field, Tiffany. 2008. Breastfeeding and antidepressants. *Infant Behavioral Development* 31 (3): 481–487.

Fildes, Valerie A. 1989. *Breasts, bottles, and babies.* Edinburgh: Edinburgh University Press.

Forbes, Bettina. 2009. ABC News: Get your facts straight on costs of low breastfeeding rates. BestForBabes.org. April 6. www.bestforbabes.org/2010/04/abc-news-get-your-facts-straight-on-costs-of-low-breastfeeding-rates/ (accessed April 6, 2009).

Foster, S. F., P. Slade, and K. Wilson. 1996. Body image, maternal fetal attachment, and breast feeding. *Journal of Psychosomatic Research* 41 (2): 181–184.

Freed, Gary L., Sarah J. Clark, Jacob A. Lohrm, and James R. Sorenson. 1995. Pediatrician involvement in breast-feeding promotion: A national study of residents and practitioners. *Pediatrics* 96 (3): 490–494.

Gallup, Gordon G., Jr., R. Nathan Pipitone, Kelly J. Carrone, and Kevin L. Leadholm. 2010. Bottle feeding simulates child loss: Postpartum depression and evolutionary medicine. *Medical Hypotheses* 74 (1): 174–176.

Galtry, Judith. 2000. Extending the "bright line": Feminism, breastfeeding and the workplace in the United States. *Gender and Society* 14:295–317.

Gane-McCalla, Casey. 2011. Michelle Obama promotes breastfeeding. News One. February 15. http://newsone.com/nation/casey-gane-mccalla/michelle-obama-promotes-breastfeeding/ (accessed February 2011).

Gates, Amy. 2010. Fox News says infant co-sleeping deaths linked to formula feeding. BlogHer. May 14. www.blogher.com/fox-news-says-infant-cosleeping-deaths-linked-formula-feeding?from=top (accessed May 2010).

Geddes, Donna T. 2007. Inside the lactating breast: The latest anatomy research. *Journal of Midwifery and Women's Health* 52:556–563.

Gilbert, Daniel T., Susan T. Fiske, and Gardner Lindzey. 1998. *The handbook of social psychology,* vol. 2. 4th edition. New York: McGraw Hill.

Golden, Janet. 2001. *A social history of wet nursing in America: From breast to bottle.* Colombus: Ohio State University Press.

———. 2010. Interview with the author. Bala Cynwyd, PA, August 2.

Goldin, Rebecca. 2009a. Interview with the author. Fairfax, VA, September 21.

———. 2009b. Spinning heads and spinning news: How a lack of statistical proficiency affects media coverage. STATS.org. October 8. http://stats.org/stories/2009/lack_stats_affects_media_oct8_09.html (accessed May 2010).

Goldin, Rebecca, Emer Smyth, and Andrea Foulkes. 2006. What science really says about the benefits of breast-feeding (and what the New York Times didn't tell you). STATS.org. June 20. www.stats.org/stories/breast_feed_nyt_jun_20_06.htm (accessed April 2009).

Graff, E. J. 2007. The mommy war machine. *Washington Post,* April 29.

Graham, Jennifer. 2006. The formula follies. *Wall Street Journal,* July 21, W11.

Granju, Katie Allison. 1998. What every parent should know about infant formula. Breastfeeding.com. www.breastfeeding.com/reading_room/what_should_know_formula.html (accessed January 2011).

———. 2004. The milky way of doing business. http://www.drjaygordon.com/development/bf/milky.asp (accessed October 9, 2009).

Greenberg, Susan H. 1999. Nursing trouble. *Newsweek,* March 7. www.newsweek.com/1999/03/06/nursing-trouble.html.

Greene, Alan. N.d. Antidepressants and nursing. www.drgreene.com/qa/antidepressants-and-nursing (accessed September 2010).

Greer, Frank R., Scott H. Sicherer, and A. Wesley Burks. 2008. Effects of early nutritional interventions on the development of atopic disease in infants and children: The role of maternal dietary restriction,breastfeeding, timing of introduction of complementary foods, and hydrolyzed formulas. *Pediatrics* 121 (1): 2007–3022.

Gribble, Karleen D., and Nina J. Berry. 2011. Emergency preparedness for those who care for infants in developed country contexts. *International Breastfeeding Journal* 6 (16). www.internationalbreastfeedingjournal.com/content/6/1/16 (accessed March 2012).

Gross-Loh, Christine. 2004. Breastfeeding, biomonitoring and the media. *Mothering Magazine,* January/February. http://mothering.com/breastfeeding/breastfeeding-biomonitoring-and-the-media (accessed March 2012).

H.E.A.L.T.H. 2009. The identity politics of breasts: Male lactation and the political economy of wo/man (part 1). June 11. http://eco-health.blogspot.com/2009/06/identity-politics-of-breasts-male.html (accessed August 2009).

Haggvist, Anna-Pia, Anne Lisa Brantsaeter, Andrej M Grjibovski, Elisabet Helsing, Helle Margrete Meltzer, and Margaretha Haugen. 2010. Prevalence of breast-feeding in the Norwegian Mother and Child Cohort Study and health service–related correlates of cessation of full breast-feeding. *Public Health Nutrition* 13:2076–2086.

Haiek, Laura N., Michael S. Kramer, Antonio Ciampi, and Rossana Tirado. 2001. Postpartum weight loss and infant feeding. *Journal of the American Board of Family Medicine* 14 (2): 85–94.

Hale, Thomas. 2002. Using antidepressants in breastfeeding mothers. Keynote address presented at La Leche League of Illinois Area Conference, Bloomingdale, IL. October 26. http://kellymom.com/bf/can-i-breastfeed/meds/antidepressants-hale10–02/ (accessed September 2011).

———. 2010. Podcast with Dr. Thomas Hale regarding Infant Risk Center. May. http://bymomsformoms.blogspot.com/2010/05/dr-thomas-hale-gives-us-sneak-peek-into.html (accessed June 2010).

Hanna, N., K. Ahmed, M. Anwar, A. Petrova, M. Hiatt, and T. Hegyi. 2004. Effect of storage on breast milk antioxidant activity. *Archives of Disease in Childhood—Fetal and Neonatal Edition* 89 (6): F218–F220.

Harutyunyan, Ruzanna. 2009. Bottle-feeding mimics child loss. Emax Health. August 15. www.emaxhealth.com/2/84/32867/bottle-feeding-mimics-child-loss.html (accessed September 18, 2011).

Hausman, Bernice L. 2003. *Mother's milk: Breastfeeding controversies in American culture.* New York: Routledge.

———. 2008. Women's liberation and the rhetoric of "choice" in infant feeding debates. *International Breastfeeding Journal* 3:10.

———. 2010. *Viral mothers: Breastfeeding in the age of HIV and AIDS.* Ann Arbor: University of Michigan Press.

———. 2011. Telephone interview with author. March 3.

Hausmann, Ricardo, Laura D. Tyson, and Saadia Zahidi. 2011. Global gender gap report 2011. World Economic Forum. http://reports.weforum.org/global-gender-gap-2011/ (accessed March 2012).

Hochschild, Arlie, and Anne Machung. 1989. *The second shift: Working parents and the revolution at home.* New York: Viking Press.

Horvath, T., B. C. Madi, I. M. Iuppa, G. E. Kennedy, G. W. Rutherford, and J. S. Read. 2009. Cochrane review: Interventions for preventing late postnatal mother-to-child transmission of HIV. *Cochrane Database of Systematic Reviews 2009,* no. 1 (January). http://onlinelibrary.wiley.com/doi/10.1002/14651858.CD006734.pub2/full (accessed October 2011).

Howard, Cynthia, Fred Howard, Ruth Lawrence, Elena Andresen, Elisabeth DeBlieck, and Michael Weitzman. 2000. Office prenatal formula advertising and its effect on breast-feeding patterns. *Obstetrics and Gynecology* 95 (2): 296–303.

Hrdy, Sarah Blaffer. 2009. *Mothers and others: The evolutionary origins of mutual understanding*. Cambridge, MA: Belknap Press.

Igumbor, E. O., R. D. Mukura, B. Makandiramba, and V. Chihota. 2000. Storage of breast milk: Effect of temperature and storage duration on microbial growth. *Central African Journal of Medicine* 46 (9): 247–251.

Ip, S., et al. 2007. Breastfeeding and maternal and infant health outcomes in developed countries. *Evidence Report/Technology Assessment (Full Report),* no. 153 (April): 1–186.

Isolauri, E., Y. Sütas, M. K. Salo, R. Isosomppi, and M. Kaila. 1998. Elimination diet in cow's milk allergy: Risk for impaired growth in young children. *Journal of Pediatrics* 132 (6): 1004–1009.

Isolauri, Erika, Annette Tahvanainen, Terttu Peltola, and Taina Arvola. 1999. Breast-feeding of allergic infants. *Journal of Pediatrics* 134 (1): 27–32.

Jacknowitz, Alison. 2004. An investigation of the factors influencing breastfeeding patterns. PhD dissertation. Santa Monica, CA: Pardee RAND Graduate School (PRGS) Dissertation Series.

Jansen, J., C. D. Weerth, and J. M. Riksen-Walraven. 2008. Breastfeeding and the mother-infant relationship—A review. *Developmental Review* 28 (4): 503–521.

Johnston, Carden. 2010. Interview with the author. Seattle, August 30.

Jones, Nancy Aaron. 2005. The protective effects of breastfeeding for infants of depressed mothers. *Breastfeeding Abstracts* 24 (3): 19–20.

Kaiser Family Foundation. 2010. Breastfeeding rates—Kaiser State Health Facts. www.statehealthfacts.org/comparebar.jsp?typ=2&ind=501&cat=10&sub=117&show=1040 (accessed July 2010).

Katz, Yitzhak, Nelly Rajuan, Michael R. Goldberg, Eli Heyman, Adi Cohen, and Moshe Leshno. 2010. Early exposure to cow's milk protein is protective against IgE-mediated cow's milk protein allergy. *Journal of Allergy and Clinical Immunology* 126 (1): 77–82.e1.

Kelleher, Christa M. 2006. The physical challenges of early breastfeeding. *Social Science and Medicine* 63:2727–2738.

Khan, Sheri Lyn Parpia. 2004. Maternal nutrition during breastfeeding. *New Beginnings* (La Leche League International) 21 (2): 44.

Kleiman, Karen. 2009. *Therapy and the postpartum woman.* New York: Routledge.

———. 2010. Interview with author, Rosemont, PA. August 2, 2010.

Knaak, Stephanie J. 2006. The problem with breastfeeding discourse. *Canadian Journal of Public Health* 97 (5): 412–414.

———. 2010. Telephone interview with the author. September 10.

Knox, Richard. 2009. Officials find swine flu hits minorities harder. NPR.org. August 19. www.npr.org/templates/story/story.php?storyId=112035625 (accessed November 18, 2011).

Kohen, Dora. 2005. Psychotropic medication and breast-feeding. *Advances in Psychiatric Treatment* 11:371–379.

Kolata, Gina. 2009. Picture emerging on genetic risks of IVF. *New York Times,* February 16. www.nytimes.com/2009/02/17/health/17ivf .html?pagewanted = all.

Kramer, M. S., and R. Kakuma. 2009. Maternal dietary antigen avoidance during pregnancy or lactation, or both, for preventing or treating atopic disease in the child (Review). *Cochrane Database of Systematic Reviews 2009,* no. 3.

Kramer, Michael S., et al. 2001. Promotion of Breastfeeding Intervention Trial (PROBIT). *JAMA* 285 (4): 413–420.

Kukla, Rebecca. 2006. Ethics and ideology in breastfeeding advocacy campaigns. *Hypatia* 21 (1): 157–180.

Laing, I. A., and C. M. Wong. 2002. Hypernatraemia in the first few days: Is the incidence rising? *Archives of Disease in Childhood—Fetal and Neonatal Edition* 87:F158–F162.

Lakshman, R., D. Ogilvie, and K. K. Ong. 2009. Mothers' experiences of bottle-feeding: A systematic review of qualitative and quantitative studies. *Archives of Disease in Childhood* 94 (8): 596–601.

Last, John M. 2002. Impartiality and advocacy. In *Encylopedia of public health,* by Lester Breslow. New York: Macmillan Reference USA.

Lauwers, Judith, and Anna Swisher. 2005. *Counseling the nursing mother: A lactation consultant's guide.* 4th edition. Sudbury, MA: Jones & Bartlett Learning.

Law, Jules. 2000. The politics of breastfeeding: Assessing risk, dividing labor. *Signs* 25 (2): 407–450.

———. 2010. Interview with the author. Chicago, July 26.

Lawrence, Ruth A. 1997. *A review of the medical benefits and contraindications of breastfeeding in the United States.* Maternal and Child Health Technical Information Bulletin. Arlington, VA: National Center for Education in Maternal and Child Health.

———. 1999. Storage of human milk and the influence of procedures on immunological components of human milk. *Acta Paediatrica Supplement* 88 (430): 14–18.

Layne, Linda, Sharra Vostral, and Kate Boyer, eds. 2010. *Feminist technology.* Urbana: University of Illinois Press.

Lee, Ellie, and Frank Furedi. 2005. Mothers' experience of, and attitudes to, using infant formula in the early months. School of Social Policy, Sociology, and Social Research, University of Kent. http://kent.academia.edu/EllieLee/Papers/1199326/Mothers_experience_of_and_attitudes_to_using_infant_formula_in_the_early_months (accessed March 2012).

Lee, Ellie. 2010. Telephone interview with the author. September 7.

Leon, Irving. 1998. Nature in adoptive parenting. Parenting in America. 1998. http://parenthood.library.wisc.edu/Leon/Leon.html (accessed September 18, 2011).

Lepore, Jill. 2009. Baby food: If breast is best, why are women bottling their milk? *New Yorker,* January 19.

Li, L., T. J. Parsons, and C. Power. 2003. Breast feeding and obesity in childhood: Cross sectional study. *British Medical Journal* 327 (October): 904.

Li, Ruowei, Sara B. Fein, and Laurence M. Grummer-Strawn. 2010. Do infants fed from bottles lack self-regulation of milk intake compared with directly breastfed infants? *Pediatrics* 125 (6): e1386–e1393.

LiveScience. 2010. Breastfed babies lack necessary vitamin D supplements. FoxNews.com. November 8. www.foxnews.com/health/2010/11/08/breastfed-babies-lack-necessary-vitamin-d-supplements/ (accessed November 8, 2010).

Livingstone, Verity H., Claire E. Willis, Laila O. Abdel-Wareth, Paul Thiessen, and Gillian Lockitch. 2000. Neonatal hypernatremic dehydration associated with breast-feeding malnutrition: A retrospective survey. *Canadian Medical Association Journal* 162 (5): 647–652.

Maher, Vanessa, ed. 1995. *The anthropology of breast-feeding—Natural law or social construct.* Oxford: Berg.

Maloney, Carolyn. 2009. Congresswoman Carolyn Maloney—Nursing moms help Rep. Maloney, Sen. Merkley introduce Breastfeeding Promotion Act. June. http://maloney.house.gov/index.php?option=com_content&task=view&id=1862&Itemid=61 (accessed May 2010).

Mannion, C. A., K. Gray-Donald, L. Johnson-Down, and K. G. Koski. 2007. Lactating women restricting milk are low on select nutrients. *Journal of the American College of Nutrition* 26 (2): 149–155.

Marks, Jennifer M., and Diane L. Spatz. 2003. Medications and lactation: What PNPs need to know: Where to seek appropriate information. *Journal of Pediatric Health Care* 17 (6): 311–317.

Martin, Daniel. 2009. Is the breastfeeding trend putting some babies at risk? Mail Online. February 18. www.dailymail.co.uk/health/article-1148209/Babies-breastfed-incorrectly-risk-dehydration-death.html (accessed May 2009).

Martyn, Christopher. 2011. Lactation wars (editorial column). *British Medical Journal* 342:d835.

Massachusetts Breastfeeding Coalition. 2004. Ethical conflicts delay the National Breastfeeding Awareness Campaign. January 3. http://massbreastfeeding.org/index.php/2004/ethical-conflicts-delay-the-national-breastfeeding-awareness-campaign/ (accessed June 2010).

Maushart, Susan. 2000. *The mask of motherhood.* New York: Penguin Books.

Mayo Clinic Staff. 2011. Pregnancy after 35: Healthy moms, healthy babies. MayoClinic.com. July 23. www.mayoclinic.com/health/pregnancy/PR00115 (accessed November 2, 2011).

McCarthy, Schatzi H. 2007. Panel: Experience of pregnancy, breastfeeding, mothering, and family planning. Cross-national perspectives: A case comparison of breastfeeding practices in Jamaica and the US. Presented at the Breastfeeding and Feminism Symposium. University of North Carolina, Chapel Hill.

McDowell, Margaret M., Chia-Yih Wang, and Jocelyn Kennedy-Stephenson. 2008. *Breastfeeding in the United States: Findings from the National Health and Nutrition Examination Survey, 1999–2006.* NHS Data Brief #5. www.cdc.gov/nchs/data/databriefs/db05.htm (accessed March 2010).

McGuinness-Snider, Devan. 2011. Online chat with author via Facebook.com. September 15.

McKay, Mary-Jayne. 2010. Gisele Bundchen's breastfeeding comments spark controversy. CBSNews.com. August 4. www.cbsnews.com/8301–504744_162–20012670–10391703.html (accessed March 2011).

Melville, Kate. 2010. Autism risk tripled with IVF. ScienceAGoGo.com. June 15. www.scienceagogo.com/news/20100515024655data_trunc_sys.shtml (accessed November 2, 2011).

Mennella, J. A., A. K. Ventura, and G. K. Beauchamp. 2011. Differential growth patterns among healthy infants fed protein hydrolysate or cow-milk formulas. *Pediatrics* 127 (1): 110–118.

Meyers, D. 2009. Breastfeeding and health outcomes. *Breastfeeding Medicine* 4 (Suppl 1): S13–S15.

Miller, Jeff. 2007. Breastfeeding, brain development and chemical poisons: Neuroscientist Michael Merzenich. UCSF.com. May 18. www.ucsf.edu/news/2007/05/3817/merzenich (accessed June 2009).

Mitoulas, Leon R., Jacqueline C. Kent, David B. Cox, Robyn A. Owens, Jillian L. Sherriff, and Peter E. Hartmann. 2002. Variation in fat, lactose and protein in human milk over 24 h and throughout the first year of lactation. *British Journal of Nutrition* 88 (1): 29–37.

Moffat, Tina. 1996. Breast is best? A review of the role of breastfeeding in the prevention of infectious disease. *Nexus: The Canadian Student Journal of Anthropology* 12 (1): 35–52.

———. 2011. Telephone interview with the author. March 15.

Moore, Kyle. 2010. Bellevue woman denies starving her baby daughter. King 5 News. January 27. www.king5.com/news/local/Bellevue-couple-accused-of-starving-baby-daughter-82814757.html (accessed Ocober 2010).

Morales, Tatiana. 2003. Battle over breastfeeding ads—The Early Show—CBS News. December 31. www.cbsnews.com/stories/2003/12/31/earlyshow/health/main590864.shtml (accessed June 15, 2009).

Moritz, Michael. 2010. Telephone interview with author. October 13.

Moritz, Michael L., Mioara D. Manole, Debra L. Bogen, and J. Carlos Ayus. 2005. Breastfeeding-associated hypernatremia: Are we missing the diagnosis? *Pediatrics* 116 (3): e343–e347.

Mothering.com. 2008. Discussion thread: Making formula prescription only. Mothering.com (Community Forums). September 24. www.mothering.com/community/forum/thread/972880/making-formula-prescription-only (accessed March 2011).

Murphy, Elizabeth. 2010. Quiet coercions: Medicine, morality and motherhood. Inaugural Lecture, University of Leicester.

National Public Radio. 2008. Study puts breastfeeding benefits in question. WBUR.org. April 1. www.wbur.org/npr/89271759/study-puts-breastfeeding-benefits-in-question (accessed September 2008).

Neifert, Marianne. 2009. *Great expectations: The essential guide to breastfeeding.* New York: Sterling.

Neifert, Marianne, S. DeMarzo, J. Seacat, D. Young, M. Leff, and M. Orleans. 1990. The influence of breast surgery, breast appearance, and pregnancy-induced breast changes on lactation sufficiency as measured by infant weight gain. *Birth* 17 (1): 31–38.

Nelson, Cate. 2009. Does bottle-feeding cause postpartum depression? August 17. http://ecochildsplay.com/2009/08/17/does-bottle-feeding-cause-postpartum-depression/ (accessed September 18, 2011).

New York State Department of Health, Division of Nutrition, Evaluation and Analysis Unit. 2011. *Barriers to retention among New York State WIC infants and children.* Final report. Alexandria, VA: U.S. Department of Agriculture.

Newman, Jack. 1997. When breastfeeding is not contraindicated. *Breastfeeding Abstracts* 16 (4): 27–28.

———. 2000. Breastfeeding and guilt. January. www.kellymom.com/newman/bf_and_guilt_01–00.html (accessed October 9, 2009).

Nommsen-Rivers, L. A., C. J. Chantry, R. J. Cohen, and K. G. Dewey. 2010. Comfort with the idea of formula feeding helps explain ethnic disparity in breastfeeding intentions among expectant first-time mothers. *Breastfeeding Medicine* 5 (1): 25–33.

Noonan, Mary. 2011. Telephone interview with the author. February 21.

Nursing Birth. 2009. New study hypothesizes bottle-feeding simulates child loss increasing a mother's chance of postpartum depression. September 1. http://nursingbirth.com/2009/09/01/new-study-hypothesizes-bottle-feeding-simulates-child-loss-increasing-a-mothers-risk-for-pp-depression/#comment-1925 (accessed October 5, 2009).

Oakley, Maureen Rand. 2008. The bottle, the breast, and the state: Breastfeeding rights policy and the role of grassroots and traditional women's rights groups. Paper, Department of Political Science, Mount St. Mary's University, Emmitsburg, MD.

———. 2010. Interview with the author. Frederick, MD, July 30.

O'Connor, Mary. 1998. Breastfeeding around the world: The International Code of Marketing Breast Milk Substitutes. www.breastfeedingbasics.org/cgi-bin/deliver.cgi/content/International/his_code.html (accessed October 9, 2009).

Ohlemacher, Stephen. 2010. IRS says breast pumps tax deductible expense. Yahoo!News. February 10. http://news.yahoo.com/s/ap/20110210/ap_on_re_us/us_breast_pumps_taxes (accessed February 2010).

O'Mara, Peggy. 2004. The dastardly deeds of the AAP. *Mothering Magazine,* issue 123 (March/April). http://mothering.com/the-dastardly-deeds-of-the-aap.

Osborn, D. A., and J. Sinn. 2003. Formulas containing hydrolysed protein for prevention of allergy and food intolerance in infants. *Cochrane Database of Systematic Reviews 2003,* no. 4: CD003664.

Palaniappan, Amudha, Lori Feldman-Winter, and Barry Milcarek. 2010. Barriers to breastfeeding reported by exclusively formula feeding mothers. Paper presented at the Children's Health: Climbing to New Heights—Walk among the Giants of Pediatrics Conference. San Francisco.

Palmer, Gabrielle. 2009. *The politics of breastfeeding.* 3rd edition. London: Pinter & Martin.

Palumbo, Polly. 2009. Telephone interview with author. October 27.

———. 2011. Email correspondence with author. January 31.

Parker-Hope, Tanya. 2008. Formula freebies cut breast-feeding time. NYTimes.com. March 20. http://well.blogs.nytimes.com/2008/03/20/formula-freebies-cut-breastfeeding-time/ (accessed March 2009).

Petosa, Rick. 1998. Fathers strongly influence mothers' decision to breast-feed. Ohio State University. February 24. http://researchnews.osu.edu/archive/brestfed.htm (accessed September 2010).

PhD in Parenting. 2010a. Guest post: Inside the American Academy of Pediatrics Conference. October 6. www.phdinparenting.com/2010/10/06/guest-post-inside-the-american-academy-of-pediatrics-conference/ (accessed October 7, 2010).

———. 2010b. It's not about picking on moms, it's about breaking down societal barriers. April 12. www.phdinparenting.com/2010/04/12/its-not-about-picking-on-moms-it-is-about-breaking-down-societal-barriers/ (accessed October 16, 2010).

Phend, Crystal. 2010. Medical news: Low breastfeeding rates incur billions in medical costs. MedPageToday. April 5. www.medpagetoday.com/Pediatrics/Parenting/19367 (accessed April 2010).

Piotrowski, Angeline Duran. 2009. Myth #23: Breastfeeding prevents obesity. Mommy Myth Buster. January 26. http://mommymythbuster.wordpress.com/2009/01/26/myth-23-breastfeeding-prevents-obesity/ (accessed May 2010).

Pittman, Genevra. 2010. Starting solid foods earlier linked to obesity risk. Reuters.com. February 7. www.reuters.com/article/2011/02/07/us-starting-risk-idUSTRE7161C220110207 (accessed February 7, 2010).

Pontifical Academy of Sciences and the Royal Society Working Group. 1995. *Food and nutrition bulletin. Japan.* Vatican City: United Nations University Press.

Rand, Scott E., and Amy Kolberg. 2001. Neonatal hypernatremic dehydration secondary to lactation failure. *Journal of the American Board of Family Medicine* 14 (2): 155–158.

Read, Jennifer S., and the Committee on Pediatric AIDS. 2003. Human milk, breastfeeding, and transmission of human immunodeficiency virus type 1 in the United States. *Pediatrics* 112 (5): 1196–1205.

Rebel Raising. 2011. Let's talk about breasts, baby. Again. October 6. http://rebelraising.wordpress.com/2011/10/06/lets-talk-about-breasts-baby-again/ (accessed October 25, 2011).

Renfrew Center Foundation for Eating Disorders. 2002, revised 2003. *Eating Disorders 101 Guide: A Summary of Issues, Statistics and Resources.* Downloadable from www.renfrew.org.

Replies to "Six months of exclusive breastfeeding: How good is the evidence?" 2011. British Medical Journal Online. www.bmj.com/content/342/bmj.c5955.full/reply#bmj_el_248661 (accessed February 2011).

Rippeyoung, Phyllis. 2009. Feeding the state: Breastfeeding and women's well being in context. *Journal of the Association for Research on Mothering* 11 (1): 36–48.

———. 2011. Telephone interview with the author. February 23.

Rippeyoung, Phyllis L. F., and Mary C. Noonan. 2010. Is breastfeeding truly free? The economic consequences of breastfeeding for women. Downloadable from http://paa2009.princeton.edu/download.aspx?submissionId=91391.

Rochman, Bonnie. 2011. *Time* Healthland: Is breast always best? Examining the link between breastfeeding and postpartum depression. August 5.

http://healthland.time.com/2011/08/05/do-depression-and-difficulty-breast-feeding-go-hand-in-hand/ (accessed September 18, 2011).

Rosenberg, Terry J., Julie K. Alperen, and Mary Ann Chiasson. 2003. Why do WIC participants fail to pick up their checks? An urban study in the wake of welfare reform. *American Journal of Public Health* 93 (3): 477–481.

Rosin, Hannah. 2009. The case against breastfeeding. *Atlantic Monthly*, April.

Rumbelow, Helen. 2009. Exposing the myths of breastfeeding. *The Times* (London), July 20.

Ruvalcaba, R. H. 1987. Stress-induced cessation of lactation. *Western Journal of Medicine* 146 (2): 228–230.

Sauberan, Jason B., et al. 2011. Breast milk hydrocodone and hydromorphone levels in mothers using hydrocodone for postpartum pain. *Obstetrics and Gynecology* 117 (3): 611–617.

Sauberan, Jason. 2011. Email correspondance with the author. March 3.

Schanler, Richard J., Karen G. O'Connor, and Ruth A. Lawrence. 1999. Pediatricians' practices and attitudes regarding breastfeeding promotion. *Pediatrics* 103 (3): e35.

Schubiger, G., U. Schwarz, and O. Tönz. 1997. UNICEF/WHO Baby-Friendly Hospital initiative: Does the use of bottles and pacifiers in the neonatal nursery prevent successful breastfeeding? *European Journal of Pediatrics* 156 (11): 874–877.

Schulmeister, U., I. Swoboda, S. Quircew, B. de la Hozz, M. Ollert, G. Pauliz, R. Valentak, and S. Spitzauer. 2007. Sensitization to human milk. *Clinical and Experimental Allergy* 38 (1): 60–68.

Schultz, S. T., et al. 2006. Breastfeeding, infant formula supplementation, and Autistic Disorder: The results of a parent survey. *International Breastfeeding Journal* 15 (1): 16.

Schwartz, Kendra, Hannah J. S. D'Arcy, Brenda Gillespie, Janet Boro, MaryLou Longeway, and Betsy Foxman. 2002. Factors associated with weaning in the first 3 months postpartum. *Journal of Family Practice* 51 (5): 439–444.

Science Daily. 2008. Lower-income neighborhoods associated with higher obesity rates. February 10. www.sciencedaily.com/releases/2008/02/080207163807.htm (accessed February 2010).

———. 2010. Why is breast milk best? It's all in the genes. May 13. www.sciencedaily.com/releases/2010/05/100512172342.htm (accessed May 14, 2010).

Sharick, Catherine. 2010. Breast pumping on rise as moms choose not to breast-feed. Time.com. March 11. www.time.com/time/magazine/article/0,9171,1975328–1,00.html (accessed September 21, 2011).

Shelton, Deborah L. 2009. Baby obesity: Rapid infant weight gain linked to childhood obesity. *Chicago Tribune,* March 30. http://articles.chicagotribune.com/2009–03–30/news/0903290224_1_childhood-obesity-weight-gain-birth-weight (accessed October 2010).

Shinwell, E. D., and R. Gorodischer. 1982. Totally vegetarian diets and infant nutrition. *Pediatrics* 70 (4): 582–586.

Smith, Paige Hall, Emily Taylor, and Miriam Labbok. 2007. *Proceedings of breastfeeding and feminism: A focus on reproductive health and rights.* Chapel Hill: University of North Carolina School of Public Health.

Smith, Sol. 2008. How to be a badass dad: The breastfeeding father. BadassDad.com. January 26. www.badassdad.com/2008/01/breastfeeding-father.html (accessed November 1, 2011).

Solomon, Stephen. 1981. The controversy over infant formula. *New York Times,* December 6.

Sonkin, Daniel. 2005. Attachment theory and psychotherapy. *California Therapist* 17 (1): 69–77.

Sonoma County Breastfeeding Coalition and Sonoma County Perinatal Alcohol and Other Drug Action Team. 2008. Counseling guidelines: Breastfeeding and maternal alcohol, tobacco and other drug use. County Counseling Guidelines, Sonoma.

Specker, Bonny L. 1994. Nutritional concerns of lactating women consuming vegetarian diets. *American Journal of Clinical Nutrition* 59 (5): 1182S–1186S.

Specker, B. L., A. Black, L. Allen, and F. Morrow. 1990. Vitamin B-12: Low milk concentrations are related to low serum concentrations in vegetarian women and to methylmalonic aciduria in their infants. *American Journal of Clinical Nutrition* 52 (6): 1073–1076.

Specker, Bonny L., Howard E. Wey, and Donald Miller. 1987. Differences in fatty acid composition of human milk in vegetarian and nonvegetarian women: Long-term effect of diet. *Journal of Pediatric Gastroenterology and Nutrition* 6 (5): 764–768.

Speisel, Sydney. 2006. Rethinking the health benefits of breastfeeding. Slate .com. March 27. www.slate.com/id/2138629/ (accessed Sept 25, 2011).

———. 2007. Breast-feeding and weight, and the new Pill. Slate.com. May 3. www.slate.com/id/2165562 (accessed August 2010).

Stapleton, Helen, Anna Fielder, and Mavis Kirkham. 2008. Breast or bottle? Eating disordered childbearing women and infant-feeding decisions. *Maternal and Child Nutrition* 4 (2): 106–120.

Stenson, Jacqueline. 2003. Do IVF kids face more health risks? MSNBC .com. July 21. www.msnbc.msn.com/id/3076781/ns/health-special_reports/t/do-ivf-kidsface-morehealth-risks/ (accessed November 2, 2011).

Stuebe, Alison. 2009. Does breastfeeding prevent postpartum depression? April 18. http://bfmed.wordpress.com/2010/04/18/does-breastfeeding-prevent-postpartum-depression (accessed May 2009).

———. 2010. When lactation doesn't work. April 24. http://bfmed .wordpress.com/2010/04/24/when-lactation-doesnt-work/ (accessed May 2010)

Stuebe, Alison M., Janet W. Rich-Edwards, Walter C. Willett, JoAnn E. Manson, and Karin B Michels. 2005. Duration of lactation and incidence of type 2 diabetes. *JAMA* 294 (20): 2601–2610.

Stuebe, Alison M., Walter C. Willett, Fei Xue, and Karin B. Michels. 2009. Lactation and incidence of perimenopausal breast cancer. *Archives of Internal Medicine* 169 (15): 1364–1371.

Symposia on breastfeeding and feminism. 2011. University of North Carolina, School of Public Health. January 12. www.sph.unc.edu/mch/symposium_on_breastfeeding__feminism_5130_4470.html (accessed January 2011).

Taubes, Gary. 2008. An interview with Walter Willet. Science Watch. http://archive.sciencewatch.com/interviews/walter_c_willett.htm (accessed November 2010).

The case against breastfeeding—Comments. 2009. Atlantic Monthly Online. April. www.theatlantic.com/magazine/archive/2009/04/the-case-against-breast-feeding/7311/ (accessed September 2010).

Third Annual Symposium on Breastfeeding and Feminism: Proceedings. 2008. University of North Carolina, School of Public Health. December 2. www.sph.unc.edu/mch/third_annual_symposium_on_breast feeding_and_feminism_proceedings_6653.html (accessed May 2010).

Thompson, Tracey. 1998. The mommy wars. *Washington Post Magazine,* February 15, W12.

Tohotoa, Jenny, Bruce Maycock, Yvonne L. Hauck, Peter Howat, Sharyn Burns, and Colin W. Binns. 2009. Dads make a difference: An exploratory study of paternal support for breastfeeding in Perth, Western Australia. *International Breastfeeding Journal* 4: 15.

Toronto Public Health. 2010. Breastfeeding in Toronto—Promoting supportive environments. www.toronto.ca/health/breastfeeding/environments_report/ (accessed March 2012).

Troy, Lisa M., Karin B. Michels, David J. Hunter, Donna Spiegelman, Joanne Manson, Graham A. Colditz, Meir J. Stampfer, and Walter C. Willet. 1996. Self-reported birthweight and history of having been breastfed among younger women: An assessment of validity. *International Journal of Epidemiology* 25 (1): 122–127.

Tufts–New England Medical Center Evidence-Based Practice Center. 2007. *Evidence report/technology assessment: Breastfeeding and maternal and infant health in developed countries: Evidence report.* AHRQ Publication no. 07-E007. Rockville, MD: Agency for Healthcare Research and Quality—Department of Health and Human Services.

Tully, Douglas B., Frances Jones, and Mary Rose Tully. 2001. Donor milk: What's in it and what's not. *Journal of Human Lactation* 17 (2): 152–155.

UNICEF. 1990. Innocenti declaration on the protection, promotion, and support of breastfeeding. www.unicef.org/programme/breastfeeding/innocenti.htm (accessed October 2009).

UNICEF Press Centre. 2003. Lack of clean water robs children of health, education. UNICEF.org. March 10. www.unicef.org/media/media_7596.html (accessed November 18, 2011).

United States Breastfeeding Committee. 2009. Letters to the editor of the *Atlantic.* United States Breastfeeding Committee. May. www.usbreastfeeding.org/LegislationPolicy/ActionCampaigns/LetterstotheEditoroftheAtlantic/tabid/116/ctl/Login/Default.aspx?returnurl=%2fLegislationPolicy%2fActionCampaigns%2fLetterstotheEditoroftheAtlantic%2ftabid%2f116%2fDefault.aspx (accessed May 2009).

University of Melbourne. 2005. Press release: Call for action on static breastfeeding rates. News—The University of Melbourne. May 9.

http://uninews.unimelb.edu.au/view.php?articleID=2322 (accessed January 2011).

U.S. Census Bureau. 2008. Maternity leave and employment patterns of first-time mothers 1961–2003. February. www.census.gov/prod/2008pubs/p70–113.pdf (accessed March 2011).

U.S. Department of Agriculture, Food and Nutrition Service. 2011. WIC—Breastfeeding promotion and support. Food and Nutrition Service—USDA. October 12. www.fns.usda.gov/wic/breastfeeding/mainpage.HTM (accessed November 18, 2011).

U.S. Department of Health and Human Services. 2011. The Surgeon General's call to action to support breastfeeding. January 20. http://www.surgeongeneral.gov/topics/breastfeeding/calltoactiontosupportbreastfeeding.pdf (accessed January 2011).

U.S. Department of Labor, Bureau of Labor Statistics. 2011. Employment characteristics of families summary. March 24. www.bls.gov/news.release/famee.nro.htm (accessed March 25, 2011).

U.S. Department of Labor, Wage and Hour Division. 2010. *Fact sheet #73: Break time for nursing mothers under the FLSA.* Washington, DC: U.S. Department of Labor.

Valenti, Jessica. 2007. *Full frontal feminism: A young woman's guide to why feminism matters.* Berkeley: Seal Press.

———. 2011. Why breastfeeding supremacists can suck my left one. October 5. http://jessicavalenti.tumblr.com/post/11071664621/why-breastfeeding-supremacists-can-suck-my-left-one (accessed November 15, 2011).

Van Esterik, Penny. 2002. Contemporary trends in infant feeding research. *Annual Review of Anthropology* 31:257–278.

Velasquez, Manuel G. 1992. *Business ethics: Concepts and cases.* 3rd edition. Englewood Cliffs, NJ: Prentice Hall.

Walsh, Wendy. 2009. The secret war against breastfeeding. August 26. www.momlogic.com/2009/08/the_secret_war_against_breastfeeding.php (accessed August 2009).

Weiten, Wayne. 2008. *Psychology: Themes and variations.* Florence, KY: Cengage Learning.

Wells, Jonathan. 2006. The role of cultural factors in human breastfeeding: Adaptive behaviour or biopower? *Human Ecology,* special issue 14 (Kamla-Raj): 39–47.

Wiessinger, Diane. 1996. Watch your language. *Journal of Human Lactation* 12 (1): 1–4.

Williams, Joan C. 2010. *Reshaping the work-family debate: Why men and class matter.* Cambridge, MA: Harvard University Press.

Wolf, Jacqueline. 2007. Panel: Women's personal liberty; Got milk? Not in public! Presented at Breastfeeding and Feminism Symposium. University of North Carolina, Chapel Hill.

Wolf, Joan B. 2007. Is breast really best? Risk and total motherhood in the National Breastfeeding Awareness Campaign. *Journal of Health Politics, Policy, and Law* 32 (4): 595–636.

———. 2010a. *Is breast best? Taking on the breastfeeding experts and the new high stakes of motherhood.* New York: New York University Press.

———. 2010b. Telephone interview with the author. August 23.

World Health Organization. 1981. International code of marketing of breast-milk substitutes. www.who.int/nutrition/publications/code_english.pdf.

———. 2010. *Guidelines on HIV and infant feeding 2010: Principles and recommendations for infant feeding in the context of HIV and a summary of evidence.* Guidelines/Recommendations. Geneva: World Health Organization.

———. N.d. Infant and young child feeding: Model chapter for textbooks for medical students. Geneva: World Heath Organization.

Wrotniak, Brian H., Justine Shults, Samantha Butts, and Nicolas Stettler. 2008. Gestational weight gain and risk of overweight in the offspring at age 7 y in a multicenter, multiethnic cohort study. *American Journal of Clinical Nutrition* 87 (6): 1818–1824.

Yang, L., and K. H. Jacobsen. 2008. A systematic review of the association between breastfeeding and breast cancer. *Journal of Women's Health (Larchmont)* 17 (10): 1635–1645.

Young, Lauren. 2009. The motherhood penalty: Working moms face pay gap vs. childless peers. *Bloomberg BusinessWeek,* June 5. www.businessweek.com/careers/workingparents/blog/archives/2009/06/the_motherhood.html (accessed March 2011).

Zuniga, Marielena. 2008. The breastfeeding battle. *Soroptomist Best for Women Magazine,* Dec/Jan/Feb, 12–17.